Summer Bridge Math
Grades 3–4

Editor: Sandra Toland
Layout Design: Tiara Reynolds
Inside Illustrations: Nathan Aaron, Mike Duggins, Ray Lambert, Wayne Miller, Tiara Reynolds
Cover Design: Chasity Rice
Cover Illustration: Wayne Miller

© 2007, Rainbow Bridge Publishing, Greensboro, North Carolina 27425. The purchase of this material entitles the buyer to reproduce worksheets and activities for classroom use only—not for commercial resale. Reproduction of these materials for an entire school or district is prohibited. No part of this book may be reproduced (except as noted above), stored in a retrieval system, or transmitted in any form or by any means (mechanically, electronically, recording, etc.) without the prior written consent of Rainbow Bridge Publishing.

Printed in the USA • All rights reserved.   ISBN 978-1-60022-452-2

Table of Contents

How to Use This Book 2	Time and Money 37
Assessment 3	Fractions and Decimals. 44
Assessment Analysis. 5	Measurement 62
Incentive Contract. 6	Charts and Graphs 67
Numeration 7	Geometry. 72
Addition and Subtraction. 12	Problem Solving 85
Multiplication and Division 23	Answer Key 93

How to Use This Book

The *Summer Bridge Math* series is designed to help children improve their mathematical skills during the summer months and between grades. *Summer Bridge Math* includes several extra components to help make your child's study of mathematics easier and more inviting.

For example, an **Assessment** test has been included to help you determine your child's mathematical knowledge and what skills need improvement. Use this test, as well as the **Assessment Analysis**, as a diagnostic tool for those areas in which your child may need extra practice.

Furthermore, the **Incentive Contract** will motivate your child to complete the work in *Summer Bridge Math*. Together, you and your child choose the reward for completing specific sections of the book. Check off the pages that your child has completed, and he or she will have a record of his or her accomplishment.

Examples are included for each new skill that your child will learn. The examples are located in red boxes at the top of the pages. On each page, the directions refer to the example your child needs to complete a specific type of activity.

Assessment

Write each number in the correct column.

A. Even   10   Odd   B. Even   6   Odd

    _____   21   _____   _____   9   _____

    _____   39   _____   _____   18   _____

    _____   42   _____   _____   27   _____

                 72   88

                 91   95

Write each number in expanded form.

C. 3,242 _____

D. 743 _____

E. 10,806 _____

Write > or < to compare the numbers.

F. 465 ◯ 312   193 ◯ 198   17 ◯ 20

G. $\frac{1}{5}$ ◯ $\frac{1}{2}$ 0.4 ◯ 0.2   1,000 ◯ 999

Use the underlined digit to round to the greatest place value.

H. 5<u>7</u> = _____   4<u>8</u>1 = _____   5<u>0</u>2 = _____

Solve each problem.

I.   3,208 $8.72   325,202   1,631
   + 2,603   + 0.65   + 43,119   + 800

J.   593   7,649   600 $18.05
    − 76   − 3,202   − 219   − 1.32

Assessment (continued)

Solve each problem.

K. 424 $0.87   3)680   22)1,804
   x 19   x   22

L.    What time is it? _____

What time will it be in 40 minutes? _____

What time was it 3 hours and 5 minutes earlier? _____

M. Jon has a 1-dollar bill, 4 quarters, 1 dime, 2 nickels, and 3 pennies in his pocket. What is the total amount of money that Jon has in his pocket?

_____

Reduce to lowest terms.

N. $\frac{4}{8}$ = _____ $\frac{6}{36}$ = _____ $\frac{5}{25}$ = _____ $\frac{11}{2}$ = _____

Find the perimeter.   **Find the area.**   **Find the volume.**

O.   8 ft.   P.   7 ft.   Q.
    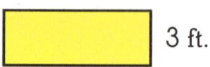 3 ft.    6 ft.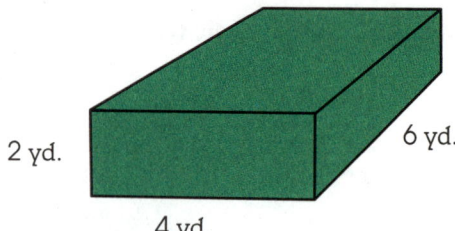
                                                                 2 yd.   6 yd.
   P = _____ ft.   4 yd.

                                  A = _____ sq. cm.

                                                              V = _____ cu. yds.

Solve.

R. Michael's class read 37 books one week, 43 books the next week, and 28 books the week after that. How many books did Michael's class read in all?

_____ books

Summer Bridge Math RB-904088   © Rainbow Bridge Publishing

Assessment Analysis

Assessment Answer Key

A. Even: 10, 42, 72; Odd: 21, 39, 91
B. Even: 6, 18, 88; Odd: 9, 27, 95
C. 3,000 + 200 + 40 + 2
D. 700 + 40 + 3
E. 10,000 + 0 + 800 + 0 + 6
F. >, <, <
G. <, >, >
H. 60, 500, 500
I. 5,811; $9.37; 368,321; 2,431
J. 517; 4,447; 381, $16.73
K. 8,056; $19.14, 226 r2, 82
L. 8:00, 8:40, 4:55
M. $2.23
N. $\frac{1}{2}, \frac{1}{6}, \frac{1}{5}, 5\frac{1}{2}$
O. 22
P. 42
Q. 48
R. 108 books

After reviewing the Assessment test, match the problems answered incorrectly to the corresponding activity pages. Your child should spend extra time on those activities to strengthen his or her math skills.

Diagnostic Problem	Review Section	Review Pages
A., B., C., D., E., F., G., H.	Numeration	7–11
I., J.	Addition and Subtraction	12–22
K.	Multiplication and Division	23–36
L., M.	Time and Money	37–43
N.	Fractions and Decimals	50–67
O., P., Q.	Geometry	68–80
R.	Problem Solving	85–92

Summer Bridge Math RB-904088   © Rainbow Bridge Publishing

Incentive Contract

		Numeration	√	My Incentive Is:
7		Ordering Numbers		
8		Writing in Expanded Form		
9		Expanded Numbers		
10		Comparing Numbers		
11		Rounding		

		Addition and Subtraction	√	My Incentive Is:
12		Addition with Regrouping		
13		Addition with Multiple Regrouping		
14		Column Addition Riddle		
15		Adding Large Numbers		
16		Subtraction with Regrouping		
17		Subtracting with Zeroes		
18		Three- and Four-Digit Subtraction		
19		Subtraction with Multiple Regrouping		
20		Mixed Practice Number Puzzle		
21		Adding and Subtracting Money		
22		Using Parentheses		

		Multiplication and Division	√	My Incentive Is:
23		Understanding Multiplication		
24		Multiplication Riddles		
25		Multiplication with Two-Digit Factors		
26		Multiplication with Regrouping		
27		Multiplying Larger Numbers		
28		Multiplying Money		
29		Understanding Division		
30		Basic Division		
31		Zeroes in the Quotient		
32		Larger Quotients		
33		Division with Remainders		
34		Larger Quotients with Remainders		
35		Dividing by Two Digits		
36		Fact Families		

		Time and Money	√	My Incentive Is:
37		Telling Time to Five-Minute Intervals		
38		Drawing Hands on Clocks		
39		Elapsed Time		
40		The Value of Money		
41		Comparing Coins		
42		Calculating Change		
43		Money Practice		

		Fractions and Decimals	√	My Incentive Is:
44		Equivalent Fractions		
45		Comparing Fractions		
46		Comparing Fractions Practice		
47		Reducing Fractions to Lowest Terms		
48		Mixed Numbers		
49		Adding and Subtracting Fractions		
50		Adding Fractions with Unlike Denominators		
51		Subtracting Fractions with Unlike Denominators		
52		Finding Fractions of Whole Numbers		
53		Using Decimals		
54		Sequencing Decimals		
55		Comparing Decimals		
56		Rounding Decimals		
57		Adding Decimals		
58		Subtracting Decimals		
59		Decimals with Different Place Values		
60		Tenths		
61		Hundredths		

		Measurement	√	My Incentive Is:
62		Capacity and Weight in the Standard System		
63		Capacity in the Metric System		
64		Weight in the Metric System		
65		Length in the Standard System		
66		Length in the Metric System		

		Charts and Graphs	√	My Incentive Is:
67		Pictographs and Bar Graphs		
68		Circle Graphs and Line Graphs		
69		Points on a Grid		
70		Using a Thermometer		
71		Using a Calendar		

		Geometry	√	My Incentive Is:
72		Symmetry		
73		Shapes		
74		Polygons		
75		Similar and Congruent Figures		
76		Labeling Congruency and Movements		
77		Solid Figures		
78		Line Segments, Lines, and Rays		
79		Angles		
80		Identifying Parts of Shapes		
81		Perimeter		
82		Area		
83		Perimeter and Area Practice		
84		Volume		

		Problem Solving	√	My Incentive Is:
85		Addition and Subtraction		
86		Multiplication		
87		Division		
88		Choosing the Operation		
89		Too Much Information		
90		Time		
91		Money		
92		Using a Pattern		

© Rainbow Bridge Publishing

Ordering Numbers

numeration

To find the order of numbers, compare their **place value** columns. Order from greatest to least:

The same numeral is in the hundreds, so move to the tens.

347	(3)
268	(4)—The least because it has a 2 in the hundreds place.
363	(2)—The second greatest because its tens place is bigger.
1,619	(1)—The greatest because it has 4 digits

Study the example above. Then, write the numbers in order from greatest to least.

A. | 172 | 905 | 730 | 340 |

905, 730, 340, 172

B. | 1,170 | 2,314 | 800 | 512 |

2,314, 1,170, 800, 512

C. | 982 | 4,000 | 960 | 6,000 |

6,000, 4,000, 982, 960

D. | 401 | 472 | 436 | 490 |

490, 472, 436, 401

Write the numbers in order from least to greatest.

E. | 87 | 107 | 71 | 17 |

17, 71, 87, 107

F. | 96 | 906 | 600 | 19 |

19, 96, 600, 906

G. | 1,900 | 2,700 | 7,000 | 4,350 |

1,900, 2,700, 4,350, 7,000

H. | 620 | 6,200 | 200 | 2,600 |

200, 620, 2,600, 6,200

Writing in Expanded Form

numeration

The place value system is based on groups of ten. This chart shows how the **ones**, **tens**, **hundreds**, and **thousands** relate to each other.

1,000	100	10	1
1 thousand = 10 hundreds	1 hundred = 10 tens	1 ten = 10 ones	one

This chart is helpful when writing numbers in expanded form. **Example:** 3,649 = 3,000 + 600 + 40 + 9

Study the example above. Then, write each number in expanded form.

			1,000	100	10	1
A.	9,516	=	9,000	+ 500	+ 10	+ 6
B.	2,358	=	2,000	+ 300	+ 50	+ 8
C.	1,407	=	1,000	+ 400	+ 0	+ 7
D.	921	=	0	+ 900	+ 20	+ 1
E.	7,800	=	7,000	+ 800	+ 0	+ 0
F.	3,264	=	3,000	+ 200	+ 60	+ 4
G.	5,182	=	5,000	+ 100	+ 80	+ 2
H.	614	=		+ 600	+ 10	+ 4
I.	4,073	=	4,000	+ 0	+ 70	+ 3
J.	9,530	=	9,000	+ 500	+ 30	+ 0

Expanded Numbers

numeration

Study the example on page 8. Then, write the numeral that means the same as each group of numbers.

A. 1,000 + 500 + 30 + 3 = _____

B. 5,000 + 900 + 40 + 7 = _____

C. 3,000 + 700 + 50 + 5 = _____

D. 7,000 + 400 + 70 + 9 = _____

E. 9,000 + 20 + 1 = _____

F. 3,000 + 100 + 2 = _____

G. 3,000 + 500 + 6 = _____

H. 6,000 + 90 + 8 = _____

I. 3,000 + 600 + 9 = _____

J. 1,000 + 600 + 90 + 8 = _____

Write each number in expanded form.

K. 3,456 _____

L. 7,324 _____

M. 9,152 _____

N. 3,569 _____

O. 2,431 _____

P. 4,022 _____

Comparing Numbers

numeration

> The **greater than (>)** and **less than (<)** symbols always point to the number of lesser value. Numbers of equal value use the equal sign (=).
>
> Examples: 543 > 53   24 < 359   204 = 204

Study the examples above. Then, use the symbols >, <, and = to compare each pair of numbers.

A. 61 ◯ 60   4,128 ◯ 2,199   2,145 ◯ 8,415

B. 34 ◯ 43   542 ◯ 249   809 ◯ 809

C. 24 ◯ 14   1,215 ◯ 5,187   9,214 ◯ 4,482

D. 351 ◯ 350   51,215 ◯ 51,215   814 ◯ 4,285

E. 921 ◯ 9,219   319,114 ◯ 312,546   312 ◯ 645

F. 48 ◯ 48   5,198 ◯ 426   8,249 ◯ 511

G. 92 ◯ 28   3,291 ◯ 5,982

H. 432 ◯ 396   5,214 ◯ 6,294

> Compare the year you were born with these numbers: 1,815; 1,995; 2,075.

Rounding

numeration

When **rounding** a number, always look to the digit to the right of the place to which you are rounding. If that digit is 4 or less, round down. If it is 5 or more, round up.

Examples: Nearest ten: 34 Nearest hundred: 487 Nearest thousand 2,279
34: round down to 30 487: round up to 500 2,279: round down to 2,000

Study the examples above. Then, solve each problem.

Round to the nearest ten.

LOOK RIGHT.

A. 72 _____   14 _____

B. 83 _____   49 _____

C. 55 _____   62 _____

D. 17 _____   29 _____

Round to the nearest hundred.

E. 34 _____   95 _____   G. 284 _____   561 _____

F. 68 _____   41 _____   H. 752 _____   689 _____

I. 924 _____   354 _____

J. 728 _____   192 _____

K. 827 _____   438 _____

Use the underlined digit to round to the greatest place value.

L. 2<u>1</u>,432 _____   7<u>2</u>,418 _____   5<u>8</u>1,242 _____

M. 4,<u>2</u>99 _____   6,<u>4</u>19 _____   7,<u>5</u>46 _____

N. 9,<u>7</u>21 _____   4,<u>1</u>42 _____   5,<u>9</u>48 _____

O. 3<u>8</u>,201 _____   3<u>4</u>,112 _____   6,<u>4</u>18,205 _____

11

© Rainbow Bridge Publishing   Summer Bridge Math RB-904088

Addition with Regrouping

addition and subtraction

When the answer in the ones column is greater than 9, you must **regroup**. It looks like this:

1. Add the **ones**. Regroup if needed.

$$\begin{array}{r} 1 \\ 3\,8 \\ +\,2\,4 \\ \hline 2 \end{array}$$

8 + 4 = 12 ones or 1 ten 2 ones

2. Now add the **tens** column.

$$\begin{array}{r} 1 \\ 3\,8 \\ +\,2\,4 \\ \hline 6\,2 \end{array}$$

Study the example above. Then, find each sum by regrouping from the ones column to the tens column.

A.   57   36   73   39   14   35
      + 28   + 46   + 17   + 29   + 14   + 15

When the sum in the tens column is greater than 9, regroup to the hundreds column. Repeat this to regroup the numbers to the end. It looks like this:

1. Add the **ones** column. Regroup if needed.

$$\begin{array}{r} 1 \\ 1\,7\,2 \\ +\,4\,7\,3 \\ \hline 5 \end{array}$$

2. Add the **tens** column. Regroup if needed.

$$\begin{array}{r} 1 \\ 1\,7\,2 \\ +\,4\,7\,3 \\ \hline 4\,5 \end{array}$$

3. Add the **hundreds** column.

$$\begin{array}{r} 1 \\ 1\,7\,2 \\ +\,4\,7\,3 \\ \hline 6\,4\,5 \end{array}$$

Study the example above. Then, find each sum by regrouping from the tens column to the hundreds column.

B.   364   591   869   453   272
      + 271   + 186   + 80   + 364   + 96

Find each sum by continuing to regroup from the hundreds column to the thousands column.

C.   3,721   2,504   6,905   863
      + 1,455   + 712   + 492   + 914

Addition with Multiple Regrouping

addition and subtraction

Many addition problems require regrouping more than once. Continue to regroup from right to left until you can solve the problem.

Study the examples on page 12. Then, find each sum. Use the answers to crack the code. Answer the riddle.

Who drives away all of his customers?

$\overline{1,200}$ $\overline{1,211}$ $\overline{1,200}$ $\overline{820}$ $\overline{1,371}$ $\overline{4,053}$ $\overline{1,200}$ $\overline{608}$

$\overline{1,156}$ $\overline{631}$ $\overline{1,371}$ $\overline{1,080}$ $\overline{3,107}$ $\overline{631}$!

954 + 417 **I**	295 + 336 **R**	419 + 792 **T**	534 + 958 **S**
863 + 337 **A**	470 + 188 **L**	2,428 + 679 **E**	737 + 419 **D**
289 + 735 **F**	1,566 + 2,487 **C**	751 + 69 **X**	825 + 208 **P**
139 + 469 **B**	449 + 154 **N**	372 + 708 **V**	608 + 98 **M**

Column Addition Riddle

addition and subtraction

1. Add the **ones** column. Regroup by carrying the **tens** column.
```
   1
 321
 157
+243
   1
```

2. Add the **tens** column. Regroup by carrying the **hundreds** column.
```
  11
 321
 157
+243
  21
```

3. Add the **hundreds** column.
```
  11
 321
 157
+243
 721
```

Study the example above. Then, solve each problem.

A. 42   25   72   38   56
    17   43   43   42   42
   +34   +18   +18   +17   +34

B. 463   248   528   382   384
   +259   +367   +279   +478   +297

C. 215   623   742   542   523
    146   168   128   187   146
   +318   +235   +296   +364   +387

Solve each problem. Then, use the code to find the hidden message. Change each digit in each sum into a letter. Write the letters in order on the lines.

| 1 = T | 2 = B | 3 = A | 4 = H | 5 = M | 6 = ! | 7 = I | 8 = S | 9 = L |

D. 247   153   1   106   329
   +284   +325   +2   +187   +487

____ ____ __ __ __ __ __ __

Adding Larger Numbers

addition and subtraction

Study the examples on pages 12 and 14. Then, solve each problem.

A. 7,432   5,068   8,430   2,573
   + 1,298   + 2,753   + 2,193   + 1,842

B.   389   4,568   32,146   41,387
   + 64,413   + 978   + 13,927   + 2,176

C. 56,143   72,615   42,516   56,247
   + 2,478 + 23,827 + 19,827   + 17,085

D. 62,148   92,416   325,146   642,158
   + 19,382 + 13,592 + 26,328 + 51,319

Subtraction with Regrouping

addition and subtraction

> If the top number in the ones column is smaller than the bottom number in the ones column, you must regroup, or **borrow**, from the next highest place value. It looks like this:
>
> 1. Subtract the **ones** column. Regroup if needed.
>
> $$\begin{array}{r} {}^{6}\,{}^{16}\\ \cancel{7}\,\cancel{6}\\ -\;3\,8\\ \hline 8 \end{array}$$
>
> 7 tens 6 ones = 6 tens 16 ones
>
> 2. Subtract the **tens** column.
>
> $$\begin{array}{r} {}^{6}\,{}^{16}\\ \cancel{7}\,\cancel{6}\\ -\;3\,8\\ \hline 3\,8 \end{array}$$

Study the example above. Then, find each difference by regrouping from the tens column.

A.
  92   80   46   37   64   51
  − 66   − 14   − 28   − 19   − 8   − 24

> When the top number in the tens column is less than the bottom number, you must regroup from the hundreds. Repeat this to regroup the numbers to the end. It looks like this:
>
> 1. Subtract the **ones** column. Regroup if needed.
>
> $$\begin{array}{r} 6\,0\,7\\ -\,2\,8\,4\\ \hline 3 \end{array}$$
>
> 2. Subtract the **tens** column. Regroup if needed.
>
> $$\begin{array}{r} {}^{5}\,{}^{10}\\ \cancel{6}\,\cancel{0}\,7\\ -\,2\,8\,4\\ \hline 2\,3 \end{array}$$
>
> 3. Subtract the **hundreds** column.
>
> $$\begin{array}{r} {}^{5}\,{}^{10}\\ \cancel{6}\,\cancel{0}\,7\\ -\,2\,8\,4\\ \hline 3\,2\,3 \end{array}$$

Study the example above. Then, find each difference by regrouping from the hundreds column.

B.
  918   427   762   586   814
  − 176   − 95   − 290   − 192   − 483

Find each difference by continuing to regroup from the thousands column.

C.
  3,476   2,380   7,545   6,819
  − 1,703   − 600   − 1,832   − 906

Subtracting with Zeroes

addition and subtraction

Begin at the ones column. You cannot subtract from 0. Find the first digit that is 1 or greater. Borrow. Regroup. Borrow again, if necessary. Regroup. Begin subtracting from the ones column.

```
                    310 10      9            9
                              3 10 10      3 10 10
      400          400         400          400
   -  285       -  285      -  285       -  285
                     5          15          115
```

Study the example above. Then, solve each problem.

A.   508   640   250   700
   − 142   − 239   − 128   − 124

B.   700   808   3,006   6,240
   − 527   − 564 − 1,242 − 4,193

C. 9,040   7,048   3,000   9,048
 − 2,318 − 6,529   − 147   − 329

D. 6,408   5,000   8,405   4,205
 − 2,299 − 2,084   − 521   − 812

Three- and Four-Digit Subtraction

addition and subtraction

Study the examples on pages 16 and 17. Then, solve each problem.

A. 642   549   754   592
   −384   −293   −628   −328

B. 462   744   2,143   7,469
   −285   −256 −1,385 −3,873

C. 4,685 6,435 9,846   3,764
   − 928 −4,972 − 928 −1,878

D. 5,648 4,657 8,408   7,645
   −3,959 −2,879 −6,519 −3,789

Subtraction with Multiple Regrouping

addition and subtraction

> Sometimes, you must regroup more than once to subtract.
>
> ```
>        6 10                16            11 16         11 16
>     3,27̸0̸           1 6̸ 10        2 ̸6̸ 10       2 ̸6̸ 10
>    -  784          3,2̸7̸0̸         3̸,2̸7̸0̸        3̸,2̸7̸0̸
>    ──────         -  784         -  784        -  784
>         6         ──────         ──────        ──────
>                       86            486           486
> ```

Study the examples above and on pages 16–17. Then, solve each problem.

A.   3,621   4,197   2,479   5,076
    −1,283   − 468   − 890   −1,256

B.   9,616   3,804   8,941   982
    − 758   −1,192   − 173   − 497

C.   8,263   7,603   9,550   645
    −4,458   − 215   −4,229   − 187

D.   850   2,972   **Write your own subtraction problem
    − 76   − 493   that uses regrouping 2 times.**

19

Mixed Practice Number Puzzle

addition and subtraction

Fill in the number puzzle using the clues provided.

Across

A. 2,000 + 500 + 30 + 5 _____
B. 550,000 + 420 + 30 _____
C. 7,800 - 2,000 - 400 - 50 _____
D. 70,000 + 6,000 + 470 + 2 _____
E. 19,165 + 120 + 5 _____
F. 6,985 - 1,550 - 3,000 - 35 _____
G. 49,915 - 22,000 - 610 _____
H. 5,000 + 32,000 + 400 + 96 _____

Down

D. 50,000 + 22,000 + 395 + 5 _____
I. 30,000 + 8,000 + 200 + 25 _____
J. 15,448 - 7,200 - 7,100 - 2 _____
K. 50,475 - 15,000 - 200 - 50 _____
L. 55,000 + 275 + 25 + 30 _____
M. 13,565 - 9,000 - 300 - 45 _____
N. 82,690 - 40,000 - 1,000 - 420 _____
O. 77,200 - 5,000 - 100 - 10 _____

Adding and Subtracting Money

addition and subtraction

When adding and subtracting money, the **decimal point** must line up in the problem and in the sum or difference. Then, you can add or subtract. Remember to include the dollar sign ($) in your answer.

```
   $3.42         $2.58        $13.42
+   1.25      +  1.23      +   2.81
   $4.67         $3.81       $16.23
```

Study the examples above. Then, solve each problem.

A. $0.51 $3.45 $41.23 $0.94
   + 0.92   + 4.82   + 29.38   − 0.38

B. $2.75 $38.41 $423.14 $525.42
   − 1.82   − 19.24   + 180.93   + 48.29

C. $42.91 $301.24 $421.24 $500.27
   + 318.09   − 130.19   − 150.82   − 123.16

Solve each problem. Then, use the code and write the letters in order on the blanks to find out what Jeremis bought with the money he saved.

1 = E	6 = B
2 = N	7 = W
3 = Y	8 = C
4 = A	9 = I
5 = L	0 = !

D. $91.70 $80.90 $86.15
   − 49.53   − 11.07   − 1.05

___ ___ ___ ___   ___ ___ ___ ___ ___

Using Parentheses

addition and subtraction

Always complete the operation inside of the **parentheses** first. Then, solve.

Example: (18 – 10) + 7 = ☐ → 18 – 10 = 8 → 8 + 7 = 15

Study the example above. Then, solve each equation.

A. (4 + 5) + 7 = _____   7 + (4 + 5) = _____

B. 17 – (3 + 5) = _____   11 – (2 + 3) = _____

C. (7 + 7) – 8 = _____   13 – (3 + 5) = _____

D. (4 + 6) – 7 = _____   (6 + 3) + 8 = _____

E. (18 – 7) + 4 = _____   (6 + 7) – 6 = _____

F. 5 + (3 + 5) = _____   (15 – 7) + 9 = _____

G. (16 – 7) + 4 = _____   7 + (10 – 2) = _____

H. (14 – 9) + 7 = _____   8 + (6 + 3) = _____

I. 7 + (14 – 6) = _____   (17 – 9) + 4 = _____

J. (3 + 3) + 8 = _____   (20 – 10) + 5 = _____

K. (17 – 8) + 7 = _____   (4 + 8) – 7 = _____

L. 5 + (15 – 8) = _____   13 – (4 + 3) = _____

M. 16 – (4 + 5) = _____   (8 + 6) – 9 = _____

Understanding Multiplication

multiplication and division

The answer to a multiplication problem is called the **product**. The numbers being multiplied are called **factors**.

To **multiply** means to use repeated addition. It is easier to understand if you imagine equal groups, then add all of the groups together.

It looks like this:

● ● ● ●   4 + 4 + 4
● ● ● ●   3 groups of 4
● ● ● ●   3 x 4 ← factors
                12 ← product

Study the example above. Then, write an addition and a multiplication problem for each picture. Find the sum and the product.

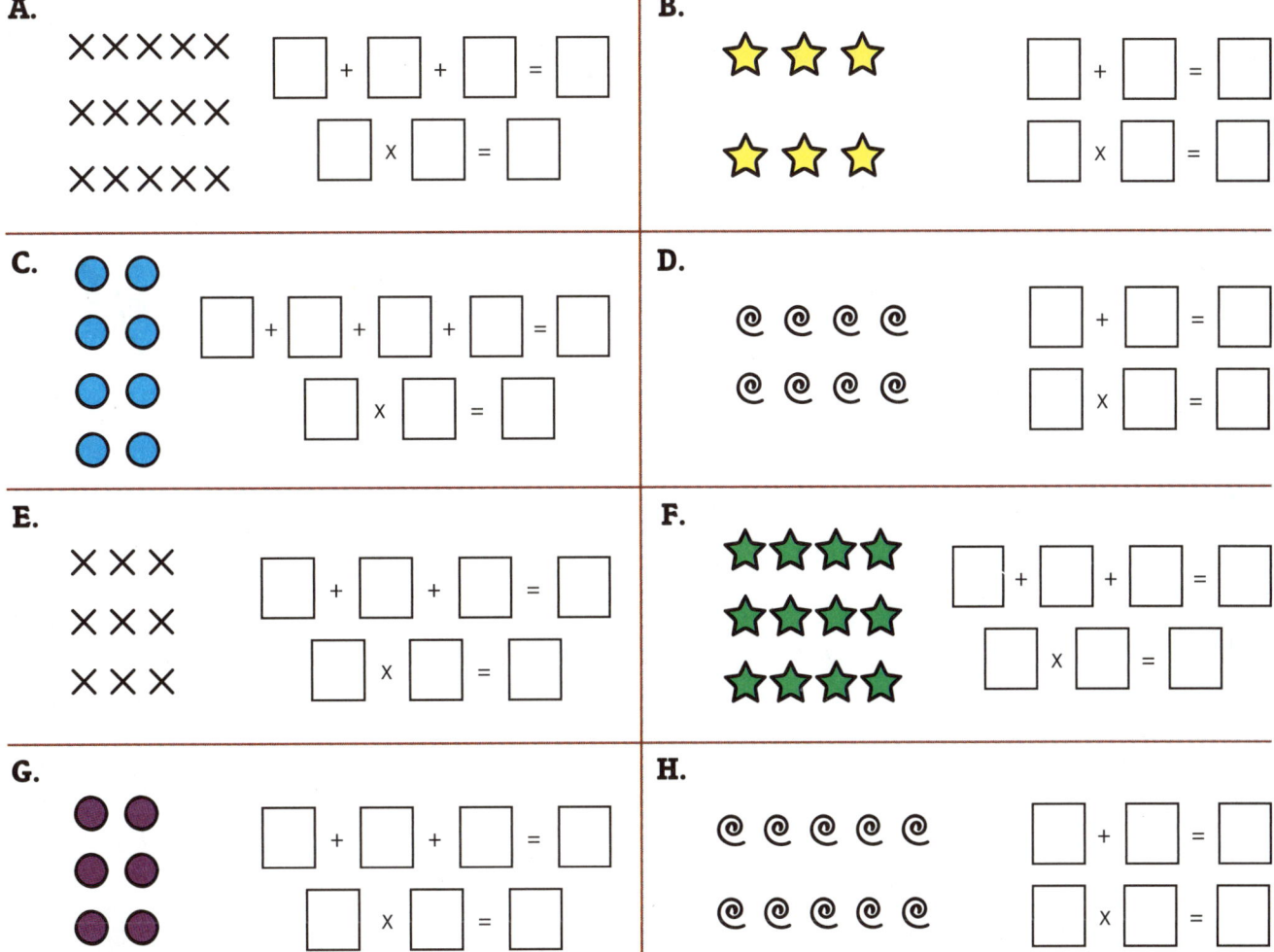

Multiplication Riddles

multiplication and division

Study the example on page 23. Then, find the products for each factor. Use the code to answer each riddle.

A	B	C	D	E	F	G	H	I	J	K	L	M	N	O	P	Q	R	S	T	U	V	W	X	Y	Z
64	4	42	7	24	16	0	18	40	11	19	49	59	25	12	13	21	56	8	54	32	28	45	60	9	14

What can you hold in your left hand but not in your right hand?

___ ___ ___ ___
3 x 3 6 x 2 8 x 4 7 x 8

___ ___ ___ ___ ___
8 x 7 5 x 8 1 x 0 6 x 3 6 x 9

___ ___ ___ ___ ___ !
8 x 3 7 x 7 2 x 2 3 x 4 9 x 5

Why is it so easy to weigh fish?

___ ___ ___ ___ ___ ___ ___
4 x 1 6 x 4 6 x 7 8 x 8 4 x 8 2 x 4 3 x 8

___ ___ ___ ___   ___ ___ ___ ___
4 x 4 8 x 5 1 x 8 9 x 2   3 x 6 8 x 8 7 x 4 4 x 6

___ ___ ___ ___ ___   ___ ___ ___
9 x 6 2 x 9 8 x 3 5 x 8 7 x 8   3 x 4 9 x 5 5 x 5

___ ___ ___ ___ ___ ___ !
4 x 2 7 x 6 8 x 8 7 x 7 6 x 4 8 x 1

24

Summer Bridge Math RB-904088

© Rainbow Bridge Publishing

Multiplying with Two-Digit Factors

multiplication and division

| 1. Multiply the ones. | 3**2**
 x **4**
 8 | 2. Multiply the bottom factor in the ones column with the top factor in the tens column. | **3**2 <br> x **4**
 128 |

Study the example above. Then, find each product.

A. 94   63   80   42
   x 2   x 3   x 8   x 3

B. 61   72   91   52
   x 9   x 2   x 7   x 4

C. 73   60   53   71
   x 3   x 6   x 2   x 5

D. 92   21   91   82
   x 4   x 9   x 8   x 2

Multiplication with Regrouping

multiplication and division

1. Multiply the ones. Regroup if needed.

    ```
      2
    265
    x   5
    ─────
        5
    ```

2. Multiply the tens. Add the extra tens. Regroup if needed.

    ```
    3 2
    265
    x   5
    ─────
       25
    ```

3. Multiply the hundreds. Add the extra hundreds.

    ```
    3 2
    265
    x   5
    ─────
    1,325
    ```

Study the example above. Then, find each product.

A.
364	378	354	671
x 2	x 2	x 3	x 4

B.
500	534	439	266
x 3	x 8	x 2	x 5

C.
180	911	236	741
x 5	x 9	x 3	x 3

D.
372	407	165	290
x 4	x 2	x 7	x 6

Multiplying Larger Numbers

multiplication and division

1. Multiply the ones.

    $$\begin{array}{r} \overset{2\,2}{\underset{3\,3}{3\,7\,8}} \\ \times\ \ \ 34 \\ \hline 1512 \end{array}$$

2. Place a zero in the ones column. Multiply by the tens digit.

    $$\begin{array}{r} \overset{2\,2}{\underset{3\,3}{3\,7\,8}} \\ \times\ \ \ 34 \\ \hline 1512 \\ +11340 \end{array}$$

3. Add.

    $$\begin{array}{r} \overset{2\,2}{\underset{3\,3}{3\,7\,8}} \\ \times\ \ \ 34 \\ \hline 1512 \\ +\ 11340 \\ \hline 129852 \end{array}$$

Study the example above. Then, find each product.

A.   310   412   362   420
   x 24   x 35   x 28   x 41

B.   543   246   185   324
   x 23   x 51   x 43   x 81

C.   624   846   231   418
   x 27   x 34   x 55   x 23

27

Multiplying Money

multiplication and division

1. Multiply.
$$\overset{2}{\cancel{x}}$$
$3.51
x   42
702
+14040
14742

2. Add the dollar ($) sign and the decimal point (.). When working with money, the decimal point goes before the second digit from the right.
$$\overset{2}{\cancel{x}}$$
$3.51
x   42
702
+14040
$147.42

Study the example above. Then, multiply. Remember to add the dollar sign and the decimal point.

A. $2.41 $3.89 $0.21 $24.12
       x   23   x   6   x   34   x   8

B. $15.41 $9.25 $0.74 $0.49
       x   3   x   34   x   51   x   21

C. $3.24 $8.54 $2.12 $0.13
       x   14   x   16   x   42   x   92

D. $0.84 $4.21 $1.98 $0.85
       x   31   x   7   x   10   x   4

Understanding Division

multiplication and division

To **divide** means to make equal groups or to share equally. The answer to a division problem is called the **quotient**. It looks like this:

Total # → 12 ÷ 3 = 4 ← # in each group
         ↑ # of groups

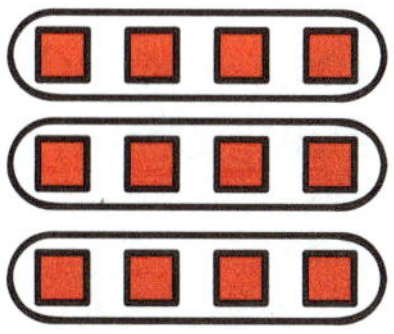

Total # → 10 ÷ 2 = 5 ← # in each group
         ↑ # of groups

Study the example above. Then, circle equal groups to find the quotient.

A.

10 ÷ 5 = ☐

B.

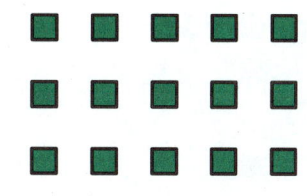

15 ÷ 3 = ☐

C.

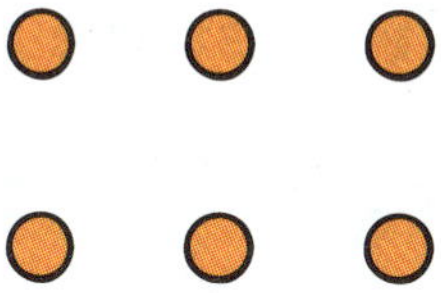

6 ÷ 3 = ☐

D.

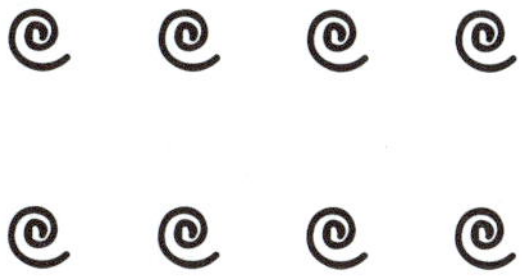

8 ÷ 2 = ☐

E.

9 ÷ 3 = ☐

F.

12 ÷ 4 = ☐

G.

12 ÷ 6 = ☐

H.

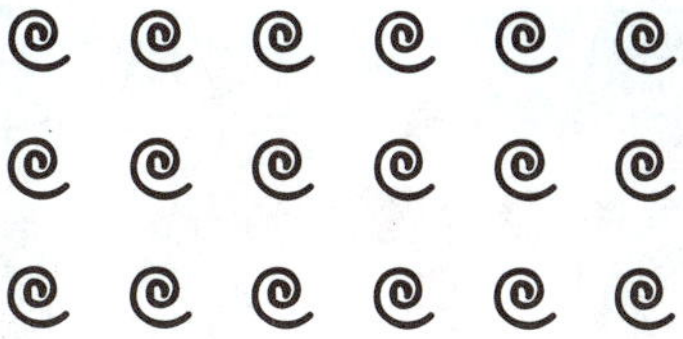

18 ÷ 3 = ☐

I.

14 ÷ 7 = ☐

Basic Division

multiplication and division

Sometimes, the **dividend** is much larger than the basic facts you have learned. In these problems you will need to do more than one step to find the quotient. Use these steps to help you:

1. Does 4 x ___ = 5? No.

    4) 56

2. Use the closest smaller dividend: 4 x 1 = 4

    ```
      1
    4)56
     -4
    ```

3. Subtract to find the remainder. Bring down the 6.

    ```
      1
    4)56
     -4↓
      16
    ```

4. Does 4 x ___ = 16? Yes! 4 x 4 = 16

    ```
      14
    4)56
     -4↓
      16
     -16
       0
    ```

Study the example above. Then, divide.

A. 6)96   2)98   5)90   7)84

B. 5)75   3)87   8)96   2)76

C. 6)84   3)54   4)96   5)85

Zeroes in the Quotient

multiplication and division

1. Is the hundreds digit great enough to divide into? Yes. Divide. Multiply and subtract.

$$\begin{array}{r} 2 \\ 3\overline{)871} \\ -6 \\ \hline 2 \end{array}$$

2. Is the difference of 2 great enough to divide into? No. Bring down the 7. Divide. Multiply and subtract.

$$\begin{array}{r} 29 \\ 3\overline{)871} \\ -6 \\ \hline 27 \\ -27 \\ \hline 0 \end{array}$$

3. Is 0 great enough to divide into? No. Bring down the 1. It is still not enough to divide into. Place a 0 in the quotient.

$$\begin{array}{r} 290 \\ 3\overline{)871} \\ -6 \\ \hline 27 \\ -27 \\ \hline 01 \\ -0 \\ \hline 1 \end{array}$$

4. Is the difference of 1 great enough to divide into? No. Are there any more digits to bring down in the dividend? No. Then, 1 becomes a **remainder**.

$$\begin{array}{r} 290\ r1 \\ 3\overline{)871} \\ -6 \\ \hline 27 \\ -27 \\ \hline 01 \\ -0 \\ \hline 1 \end{array}$$

Study the example above. Then, divide.

A. $3\overline{)925}$ $5\overline{)904}$ $2\overline{)813}$ $4\overline{)839}$ $7\overline{)985}$

B. $6\overline{)656}$ $8\overline{)966}$ $4\overline{)434}$ $2\overline{)680}$ $4\overline{)760}$

C. $2\overline{)811}$ $5\overline{)519}$ $6\overline{)845}$ $3\overline{)622}$ $6\overline{)641}$

Larger Quotients

multiplication and division

1. Is the thousands digit great enough to divide into? No. Divide into the 39 hundreds. Multiply. Subtract.

```
      9
4 ) 3,948
  - 36
     3
```

2. Is the difference of 3 great enough to divide into? No. Bring down the 4. Divide. Multiply and subtract.

```
     98
4 ) 3,948
  - 36
    34
  - 32
     2
```

3. Is the difference of 2 great enough to divide into? No. Bring down the 8. Divide. Multiply and subtract.

```
    987
4 ) 3,948
  - 36
    34
  - 32
    28
  - 28
     0
```

4. Check your answer! Multiply the quotient by the divisor. If the product matches your dividend, your answer is correct.

```
    987
  ×   4
  3,948
```

Study the example above. Then, divide.

A. 5) 4,065   3) 9,636   2) 1,968   4) 5,032

B. 6) 5,202   4) 2,560   6) 5,112   3) 1,485

C. 9) 4,923   6) 3,156   8) 1,584   4) 4,980

Division with Remainders

multiplication and division

Sometimes, when you try to make equal groups, there are numbers left over. They are called **remainders**. Use these steps to find remainders:

Find 4)18

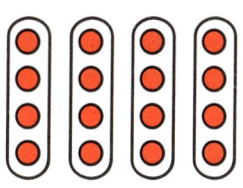

4 groups of 4 = 16
2 left over = r 2
So... 4 r2
4)18

1. Does 4 x ___ = 18
   NO!

   Think: 4 x ___ is the closest to 18?

2. Use the closest smaller dividend: 4 x 4 = 16

   ```
       4
   4)18
   - 16
      2
   ```

3. Subtract to find the remainder. The remainder is always less than the divisor

   ```
      4 r2
   4)18
   - 16
      2
   ```

Study the example above. Then, find each quotient and its remainder.

A. 8)34   4)26   7)67   3)17

B. 9)29   5)42   6)47   9)83

C. 6)39   4)19   5)24   8)79

D. 7)41   6)23   9)60   4)15

Larger Quotients with Remainders

multiplication and division

| 1. Is the thousands digit great enough to divide into? No. Divide into the 27 hundreds. Multiply and subtract. $$\begin{array}{r}6\\4\overline{)2{,}758}\\-24\\\hline 3\end{array}$$ | 2. Is the difference great enough to divide into? No. Bring down the 5. Divide. Multiply and subtract. $$\begin{array}{r}68\\4\overline{)2{,}758}\\-24\\\hline 35\\-32\\\hline 3\end{array}$$ | 3. Is the difference great enough to divide into? No. Bring down the 8. Divide. Multiply and subtract. $$\begin{array}{r}689\\4\overline{)2{,}758}\\-24\\\hline 35\\-32\\\hline 38\\-36\\\hline 2\end{array}$$ | 4. Is the difference great enough to divide into? No. Are there any more digits in the dividend to carry down? No. The 2 becomes the remainder. $$\begin{array}{r}689\text{ r}2\\4\overline{)2{,}758}\\-24\\\hline 35\\-32\\\hline 38\\-36\\\hline 2\end{array}$$ |

Study the example above. Then, divide.

A. $3\overline{)1{,}286}$ $2\overline{)6{,}843}$ $5\overline{)1{,}423}$ $4\overline{)867}$

B. $6\overline{)2{,}475}$ $5\overline{)3{,}174}$ $4\overline{)1{,}543}$ $3\overline{)9{,}367}$

C. $8\overline{)3{,}618}$ $7\overline{)1{,}730}$ $2\overline{)8{,}469}$ $6\overline{)2{,}806}$

Dividing by Two Digits

multiplication and division

1. Is the hundreds digit great enough to divide into? No. Is the 13 tens great enough to divide into? No. So, you must divide into the 137 ones.

   $21\overline{)137}$

2. How many groups of 21 are there in 137? Round the divisor to 20. Think: There are five 20s in 100. There is one more in 37. So the partial quotient must be 6.

   $\begin{array}{r}5\\20\overline{)100}\\-100\\\hline 0\end{array}$ $\begin{array}{r}1\\20\overline{)37}\\-20\\\hline 17\end{array}$

   $5 + 1 = 6$

   Think about rounding the divisor to predict the amount of the partial quotient.

3. Divide. Multiply and subtract. Is the difference less than the divisor? Yes. Then, go on.

   $\begin{array}{r}6\\21\overline{)137}\\-126\\\hline 11\end{array}$

4. Is the difference of 11 great enough to divide into? No. So, 11 becomes the remainder.

   $\begin{array}{r}6\,r11\\21\overline{)137}\\-126\\\hline 11\end{array}$

   Note: The remainder can be any amount, as long as it is less than the divisor (in this case the divisor is 21).

Study the example above. Then, divide.

A. $17\overline{)54}$ $32\overline{)130}$ $41\overline{)215}$ $11\overline{)106}$ $22\overline{)180}$

B. $49\overline{)190}$ $39\overline{)244}$ $52\overline{)436}$ $19\overline{)80}$ $61\overline{)500}$

C. $31\overline{)150}$ $78\overline{)399}$ $81\overline{)161}$ $29\overline{)223}$ $13\overline{)75}$

Fact Families

multiplication and division

A **fact family** is made up of three numbers that are related. The numbers can be used in a set of math problems. Just like addition and subtraction facts, multiplication and division facts are related.

__2__ x __3__ = __6__
__3__ x __2__ = __6__
__6__ ÷ __3__ = __2__
__6__ ÷ __2__ = __3__

Study the example above. Then, write 2 multiplication and 2 division equations for each problem.

A.

____ x ____ = ____
____ x ____ = ____
____ ÷ ____ = ____
____ ÷ ____ = ____

B.

____ x ____ = ____
____ x ____ = ____
____ ÷ ____ = ____
____ ÷ ____ = ____

C.

____ x ____ = ____
____ x ____ = ____
____ ÷ ____ = ____
____ ÷ ____ = ____

D.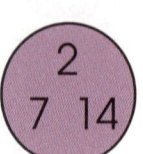

____ x ____ = ____
____ x ____ = ____
____ ÷ ____ = ____
____ ÷ ____ = ____

E.

____ x ____ = ____
____ x ____ = ____
____ ÷ ____ = ____
____ ÷ ____ = ____

F.

____ x ____ = ____
____ x ____ = ____
____ ÷ ____ = ____
____ ÷ ____ = ____

Summer Bridge Math RB-904088 © Rainbow Bridge Publishing

Telling Time to Five-Minute Intervals

time and money

The **minute hand** on a clock is the long hand. It takes 5 minutes to move from one number on the clock to the next. Therefore, we count by 5 as the minute hand moves from one number to the next. To read this clock, we say:

20 minutes past 3:00
or
3:20

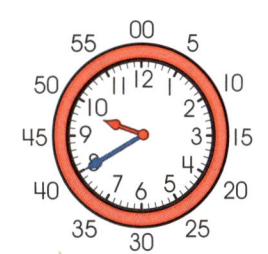

40 minutes past 9:00
or
9:40

Study the examples above. Then, write each time two ways.

A. [ ] minutes past [ ] [:]

B. [ ] minutes past [ ] [:]

C. [ ] minutes past [ ] [:]

D. [ ] minutes past [ ] [:]

E. [ ] minutes past [ ] [:]

F. [ ] minutes past [ ] [:]

G. [ ] minutes past [ ] [:]

H. [ ] minutes past [ ] [:]

I. [ ] minutes past [ ] [:]

J. [ ] minutes past [ ] [:]

Drawing Hands on Clocks

time and money

Study the examples on page 37. Then, draw hands on each clock to show the time.

A.

8:35

B.

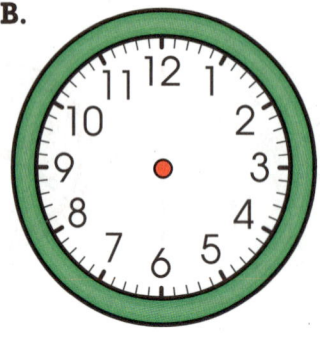

9:50

C.

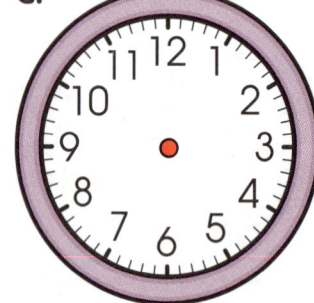

6:47

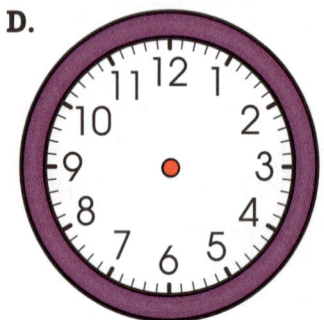

D.

12:23

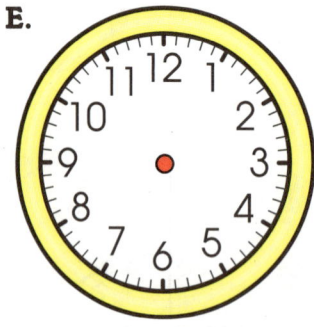

E.

10:25

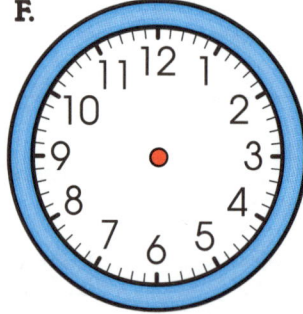

F.

7:53

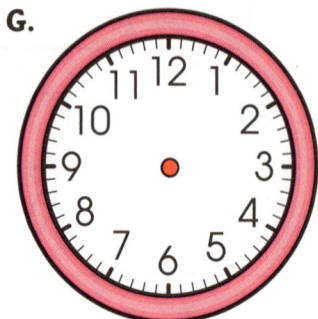

G.

11:08

H.

4:47

I.

6:17

Summer Bridge Math RB-904088

© Rainbow Bridge Publishing

Elapsed Time

time and money

To find out what time it will be later, add the **elapsed** time to the current time. **Example:** It is 10:42. What time will it be in 1 hour and 28 minutes? One hour later than 10:42 is 11:42. Twenty-eight minutes later than 11:42 is 12:10.

10:42

12:10

Study the example above. Then, use the clocks to answer each question.

A.

What time does the clock show? _____

What time would it be if it was 20 minutes earlier? _____

What time will it be in 3 hours and 35 minutes? _____

What time will it be in 65 minutes? _____

B.

What time does the clock show? _____

What time would it be if it was 48 minutes earlier? _____

What time will it be in 5 hours and 22 minutes? _____

What time will it be in 57 minutes? _____

C.

What time does the clock show? _____

What time would it be if it was 8 hours and 15 minutes earlier? _____

What time will it be in 4 hours and 15 minutes? _____

What time will it be in 75 minutes? _____

The Value of Money

time and money

These are five commonly used **coins** in the United States.

Think of a **dollar** as 100 cents. This means that each dollar is actually 100 equal parts.

50¢ or $0.50   25¢ or $0.25   10¢ or $0.10   5¢ or $0.05   1¢ or $0.01

Study the coin values above. Then, write each total value.

A. $1 bill, half dollar, penny, quarter _____

B. half dollar, half dollar, half dollar, penny, penny, penny _____

C. half dollar, half dollar, dime, penny, penny, penny _____

D. 3 $1 bills, quarter, half dollar, quarter _____

E. 5 quarters _____

F. $1 bill, half dollar, quarter, quarter _____

G. 2 $1 bills, dime, nickel _____

H. $1 bill, half dollar, half dollar, quarter, quarter _____

I. 3 half dollars _____

J. 3 $1 bills, nickel _____

Comparing Coins

time and money

Values of money can be made using different **combinations** of coins. Each group of coins below is equal.

= 25¢   = 25¢   = 25¢

Study the example above and the coin values on page 40. Then, complete each equation.

A. 5 nickels = _____ quarter

B. 50 pennies = _____ dimes

C. 1 dollar = _____ quarters

D. 4 half dollars = _____ dollars

E. 10 dimes = _____ nickels

F. 2 quarters = _____ nickels

G. 50 pennies = _____ nickels

H. 3 dollars = _____ quarters

I. 6 quarters = _____ dimes

J. 2 dimes = _____ pennies

Write two ways to make each total value.

K. $2.50 = _____ or _____

L. $1.00 = _____ or _____

M. $0.75 = _____ or _____

N. $1.25 = _____ or _____

Calculating Change

time and money

Have you ever paid for something and been given change back? The cashier figures your change using these steps:

1. Begin with the amount you paid the cashier.
2. Subtract the amount you owe from the amount you paid.
3. The difference is your change.

$$\begin{array}{r} \overset{4\ \ 9\ 10}{\$\cancel{5}.\cancel{0}\cancel{0}} \\ -\ \ \ 0.75 \\ \hline \$4.25 \end{array}$$

Study the example above. Then, find each amount of change that is owed to the customer.

A.	Paid	$6.00	**B.**	Paid	$20.00	
	Owe	− 2.10		Owe	− 16.20	
C.	Paid	$8.00	**D.**	Paid	$10.00	
	Owe	− 3.95		Owe	− 4.60	
E.	Paid	$9.00	**F.**	Paid	$5.00	
	Owe	− 8.50		Owe	− 0.95	
G.	Paid	$16.00	**H.**	Paid	$25.00	
	Owe	− 15.15		Owe	− 5.00	
I.	Paid	$2.00	**J.**	Paid	$4.00	
	Owe	− 1.19		Owe	− 3.95	
K.	Paid	$10.00	**L.**	Paid	$12.00	
	Owe	− 7.49		Owe	− 11.23	

Money Practice

time and money

Study the examples on pages 40 and 41. Then, solve each problem.

A. 4 one-dollar bills, 3 quarters, 1 dime = $_____._____

B. 5 quarters, 15 pennies, 9 one-dollar bills, 5 dimes = $_____._____

C. 6 ten-dollar bills, 3 half-dollars, 7 nickels, 1 quarter = $_____._____

D. 6 five-dollar bills, 1 half-dollar, 3 dimes, 1 one-dollar bill = $_____._____

E. 8 half-dollars, 9 nickels, 4 dimes, 3 five-dollar bills = $_____._____

Write the combination of money needed to solve each problem.

F. Write 5 coins that make a total of $1.50.

G. Write 2 bills and 7 coins that make a total of $6.27.

H. Write 9 coins and 1 bill that make a total of $2.24.

I. Write 6 bills that make a total of $40.00.

J. Write a combination of coins and bills that have a total of $9.85.

K. Write 8 coins and 3 bills that make a total of $16.30.

L. Write 15 coins and 3 bills that make a total of $8.50.

M. Write 12 bills and 11 coins that make a total of $106.69.

Equivalent Fractions

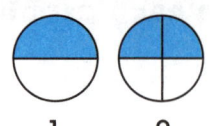

fractions and decimals

$\frac{1}{2} = \frac{2}{4}$

Fractions that equal the same amount are called **equivalent fractions**.

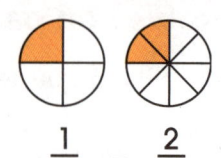

$\frac{1}{4} = \frac{2}{8}$

It is the same amount of pizza; the pieces are just different sizes!

Study the examples above. Then, write each equivalent fraction.

A. ___ = ___   ___ = ___   ___ = ___

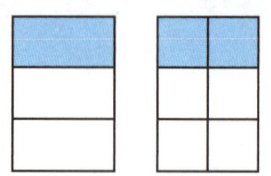

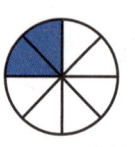

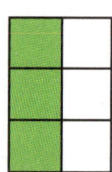

B. ___ = ___   ___ = ___   ___ = ___

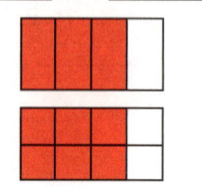

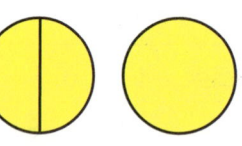

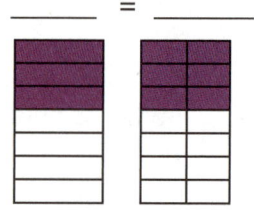

C. ___ = ___   ___ = ___   ___ = ___

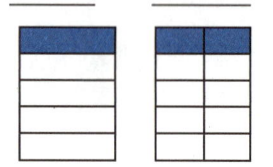

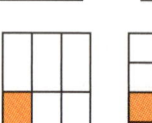

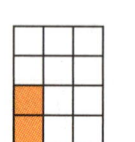

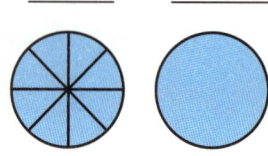

D. ___ = ___   ___ = ___   ___ = ___

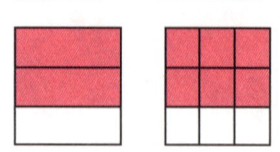

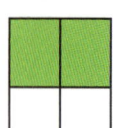

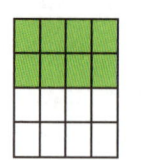

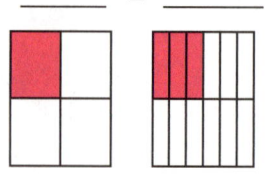

E. ___ = ___   ___ = ___   ___ = ___

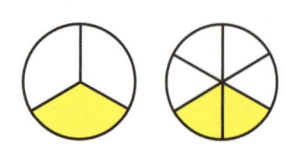

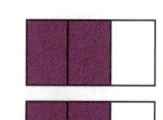

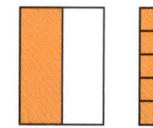

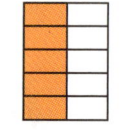

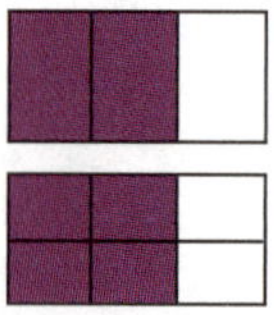

44

Summer Bridge Math RB-904088

© Rainbow Bridge Publishing

Comparing Fractions

fractions and decimals

Fractions are a way to describe equal parts of a whole. They look like this:

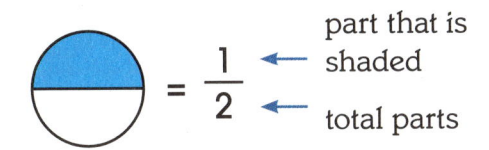

= $\frac{1}{2}$ ← part that is shaded
← total parts

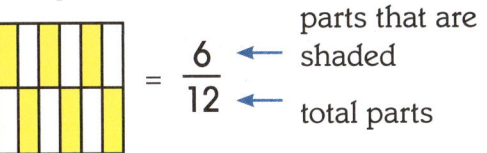

= $\frac{6}{12}$ ← parts that are shaded
← total parts

Larger numbers do not always mean larger fractions. We can compare fractions using <, >, and =.

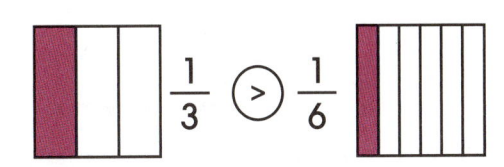

$\frac{1}{3}$ > $\frac{1}{6}$

Study the examples above. Then, write a fraction for each picture. Compare each pair of fractions using <, >, or =.

A.

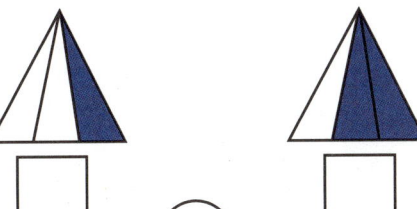

B.

C.

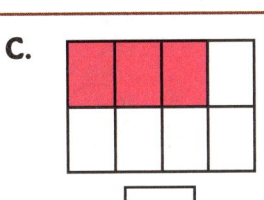

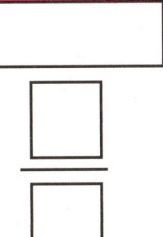

D.

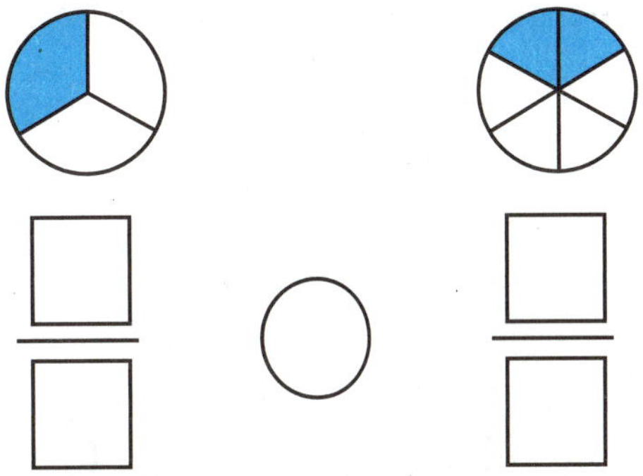

E.

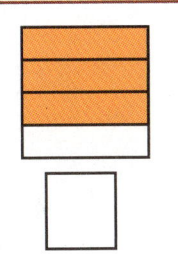

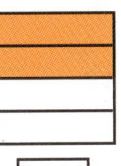

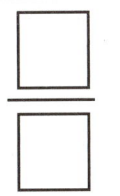

F.

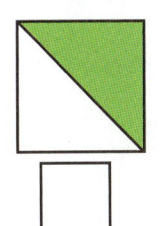

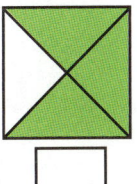

Comparing Fractions Practice

fractions and decimals

> In order to **compare**, you must find equivalent fractions.
>
> $\frac{1}{4}$ ○ $\frac{1}{8}$
>
> Multiply the numerator and the denominator by 2 to create equivalent fractions.
>
> $\frac{1 \times 2}{4 \times 2} = \frac{2}{8}$
>
> First, find a common denominator. Does something multiplied by 4 equal 8? Yes, 2. Eight is the common denominator.
>
> $\frac{1}{4} = \frac{2}{8}$
>
> Compare.
> $\frac{1}{4} = \frac{2}{8}$

Study the example above. Then, compare using >, <, or =.

A. $\frac{5}{10}$ ○ $\frac{2}{10}$ $\frac{1}{3}$ ○ $\frac{2}{3}$ $\frac{5}{8}$ ○ $\frac{6}{8}$ $\frac{3}{10}$ ○ $\frac{8}{10}$

B. $\frac{1}{4}$ ○ $\frac{3}{4}$ $\frac{6}{7}$ ○ $\frac{3}{7}$ $\frac{4}{6}$ ○ $\frac{1}{6}$ $\frac{5}{9}$ ○ $\frac{4}{9}$

C. $\frac{6}{11}$ ○ $\frac{9}{11}$ $\frac{1}{5}$ ○ $\frac{3}{5}$ $\frac{3}{4}$ ○ $\frac{2}{4}$ $\frac{2}{3}$ ○ $\frac{1}{3}$

D. $\frac{1}{2}$ ○ $\frac{3}{4}$ $\frac{1}{6}$ ○ $\frac{2}{3}$ $\frac{3}{4}$ ○ $\frac{1}{8}$ $\frac{2}{4}$ ○ $\frac{1}{2}$

E. $\frac{6}{8}$ ○ $\frac{2}{4}$ $\frac{1}{3}$ ○ $\frac{2}{9}$ $\frac{4}{6}$ ○ $\frac{2}{3}$ $\frac{1}{5}$ ○ $\frac{2}{15}$

Reducing Fractions to Lowest Terms
fractions and decimals

$\frac{6}{12}$

What is the **greatest common factor (GCF)** we can divide into both the numerator and the denominator?

$\frac{6 \div 6}{12 \div 6} = \frac{1}{2}$

6 is the GCF. Divide.

$\frac{1}{2}$

Is there a common factor greater than 1 that will divide into both of these numbers? No. The fraction is reduced to lowest terms.

If the numerator and the denominator are the same, it reduces to 1.

$\frac{3}{9} = \frac{3 \div 3}{9 \div 3} = \frac{1}{3}$ $\frac{4}{12} = \frac{4 \div 4}{12 \div 4} = \frac{1}{3}$ $\frac{8}{12} = \frac{8 \div 4}{12 \div 4} = \frac{2}{3}$

Study the examples above. Then, reduce each fraction to lowest terms.

A. $\frac{10}{12}$ = _____ $\frac{4}{16}$ = _____ $\frac{6}{18}$ = _____ $\frac{10}{15}$ = _____

B. $\frac{14}{16}$ = _____ $\frac{7}{21}$ = _____ $\frac{5}{15}$ = _____ $\frac{4}{10}$ = _____

C. $\frac{9}{18}$ = _____ $\frac{8}{24}$ = _____ $\frac{4}{8}$ = _____ $\frac{10}{16}$ = _____

D. $\frac{7}{14}$ = _____ $\frac{6}{12}$ = _____ $\frac{12}{14}$ = _____ $\frac{8}{10}$ = _____

E. $\frac{5}{20}$ = _____ $\frac{6}{24}$ = _____ $\frac{5}{25}$ = _____ $\frac{10}{40}$ = _____

Mixed Numbers

fractions and decimals

If the numerator is greater than the denominator, this type of fraction is called an **improper fraction**.

$$\frac{11}{5}$$

More examples:

$$\frac{7}{3} = 3\overline{)7} \atop -6 \atop 1 = 2\frac{1}{3}$$

An improper fraction can be written as a mixed number. Divide the numerator by the denominator. The whole number tells how many whole parts there are.

$$5\overline{)11} \atop -10 \atop 1$$

$$\frac{14}{4} = 4\overline{)14} \atop -12 \atop 2 = 3\frac{2}{4} = 3\frac{1}{2}$$

The remainder becomes the numerator. The divisor becomes the denominator.

$$5\overline{)11} \atop -10 \atop 1 = 2\frac{1}{5}$$

Study the examples above. Then, convert each fraction to a mixed number. Simplify each fraction.

A. $\frac{15}{7} =$ ___ $\frac{14}{4} =$ ___ $\frac{13}{8} =$ ___ $\frac{11}{5} =$ ___

B. $\frac{17}{9} =$ ___ $\frac{13}{4} =$ ___ $\frac{16}{5} =$ ___ $\frac{11}{2} =$ ___

C. $\frac{10}{4} =$ ___ $\frac{21}{5} =$ ___ $\frac{23}{6} =$ ___ $\frac{19}{6} =$ ___

D. $\frac{9}{2} =$ ___ $\frac{15}{6} =$ ___ $\frac{26}{6} =$ ___ $\frac{18}{8} =$ ___

E. $\frac{9}{7} =$ ___ $\frac{30}{4} =$ ___ $\frac{14}{5} =$ ___ $\frac{13}{6} =$ ___

48

Summer Bridge Math RB-904088

© Rainbow Bridge Publishing

Adding and Subtracting Fractions

fractions and decimals

The top and bottom numbers in a fraction have different meanings. They also have different names.

$\dfrac{3}{4}$ ← **numerator**
← **denominator**

To add or subtract fractions, the denominators must be the same. The denominator in the answer will also be the same. Add or subtract the numerators only.

$\dfrac{1}{3} + \dfrac{1}{3} = \dfrac{2}{3}$ ← added numerators, 1 + 1
← denominator stays the same

Study the example above. Then, solve each problem.

A. $\dfrac{2}{4} + \dfrac{1}{4} = \dfrac{\Box}{\Box}$ $\dfrac{6}{8} - \dfrac{4}{8} = \dfrac{\Box}{\Box}$ $\dfrac{1}{5} + \dfrac{3}{5} = \dfrac{\Box}{\Box}$

B. $\dfrac{4}{10} + \dfrac{5}{10} = \dfrac{\Box}{\Box}$ $\dfrac{7}{8} - \dfrac{5}{8} = \dfrac{\Box}{\Box}$ $\dfrac{9}{10} - \dfrac{3}{10} = \dfrac{\Box}{\Box}$

C. $\dfrac{6}{9} + \dfrac{2}{9} = \dfrac{\Box}{\Box}$ $\dfrac{10}{12} - \dfrac{3}{12} = \dfrac{\Box}{\Box}$ $\dfrac{2}{4} - \dfrac{1}{4} = \dfrac{\Box}{\Box}$

D. $\dfrac{68}{100} + \dfrac{12}{100} = \dfrac{\Box}{\Box}$ $\dfrac{42}{100} + \dfrac{36}{100} = \dfrac{\Box}{\Box}$ $\dfrac{25}{100} + \dfrac{75}{100} = \dfrac{\Box}{\Box}$

Adding Fractions with Unlike Denominators *fractions and decimals*

| 1. Create equivalent fractions with a common denominator. $\frac{1}{8}$ $\frac{1\times 2}{8\times 2}$ $\frac{2}{16}$ $+\frac{2}{16}$ $+\frac{8}{10}$ $\frac{2}{16}$ | 2. Add. $\frac{2}{16}$ $+\frac{2}{16}$ $\frac{4}{16}$ | 3. Reduce to lowest terms. $\frac{4\div 4}{16\div 4} = \frac{1}{4}$ |

Study the example above. Then, solve each problem. Reduce if possible.

A. $\frac{1}{5} + \frac{1}{10}$ $\frac{1}{12} + \frac{4}{6}$ $\frac{1}{7} + \frac{7}{14}$ $\frac{3}{5} + \frac{2}{15}$

B. $\frac{3}{6} + \frac{1}{3}$ $\frac{1}{4} + \frac{5}{8}$ $\frac{1}{8} + \frac{1}{2}$ $\frac{3}{7} + \frac{3}{14}$

C. $\frac{3}{10} + \frac{2}{5}$ $\frac{1}{6} + \frac{5}{12}$ $\frac{5}{10} + \frac{2}{5}$ $\frac{1}{2} + \frac{1}{4}$

D. $\frac{1}{12} + \frac{1}{6}$ $\frac{3}{10} + \frac{1}{2}$ $\frac{2}{16} + \frac{3}{8}$ $\frac{6}{9} + \frac{1}{3}$

Subtracting Fractions with Unlike Denominators — fractions and decimals

1. Create equivalent fractions with a common denominator.

$$\frac{8}{10} \quad \frac{8}{10} \quad \frac{8}{10}$$
$$-\frac{2}{5} \quad -\frac{2\times 2}{5\times 2} \quad -\frac{4}{10}$$

2. Subtract.

$$\frac{8}{10} - \frac{4}{10} = \frac{4}{10}$$

3. Reduce to lowest terms.

$$\frac{4 \div 2}{10 \div 2} = \frac{2}{5}$$

Study the example above. Then, solve each problem. Reduce if possible.

A. $\frac{3}{4} - \frac{1}{2}$ $\frac{14}{16} - \frac{5}{8}$ $\frac{4}{5} - \frac{5}{10}$ $\frac{9}{14} - \frac{3}{7}$

B. $\frac{5}{6} - \frac{2}{3}$ $\frac{1}{3} - \frac{1}{12}$ $\frac{2}{4} - \frac{1}{8}$ $\frac{1}{2} - \frac{4}{10}$

C. $\frac{7}{9} - \frac{11}{18}$ $\frac{5}{6} - \frac{9}{12}$ $\frac{4}{8} - \frac{1}{2}$ $\frac{1}{2} - \frac{1}{4}$

D. $\frac{6}{8} - \frac{1}{2}$ $\frac{3}{5} - \frac{5}{10}$ $\frac{13}{14} - \frac{6}{7}$ $\frac{3}{4} - \frac{3}{8}$

Finding Fractions of Whole Numbers

fractions and decimals

$\frac{1}{4}$ of 16

Divide the whole number by the denominator. $16 \div 4 = 4$

Multiply this quotient by the numerator. $1 \times 4 = 4$

$\frac{1}{4}$ of 12

$12 \div 4 = 3$
$1 \times 3 = 3$

The denominator tells us how many equal groups to make. The numerator tells us how many of these groups to add together.

Study the examples above. Then, solve each problem.

A. $\frac{1}{3}$ of 15 $\frac{1}{6}$ of 12 $\frac{1}{2}$ of 10 $\frac{1}{4}$ of 20

B. $\frac{1}{7}$ of 14 $\frac{1}{8}$ of 24 $\frac{1}{7}$ of 28 $\frac{1}{3}$ of 27

C. $\frac{1}{5}$ of 30 $\frac{1}{8}$ of 40 $\frac{1}{4}$ of 36 $\frac{2}{5}$ of 10

D. $\frac{1}{5}$ of 45 $\frac{2}{3}$ of 21 $\frac{4}{6}$ of 12 $\frac{1}{10}$ of 20

E. $\frac{1}{4}$ of 16 $\frac{3}{5}$ of 15 $\frac{1}{8}$ of 64 $\frac{3}{4}$ of 20

Using Decimals

fractions and decimals

Fractions that are **tenths** ($\frac{1}{10}$) or **hundredths** ($\frac{1}{100}$) can be written as a decimal. When there are no whole numbers, put a 0 in the ones place.

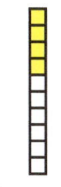

$\frac{4}{10}$ = 0.4 =
four tenths

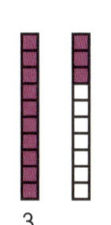

$1\frac{3}{10}$ = 1.3 =
one whole and three tenths

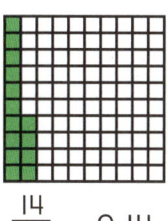

$\frac{14}{100}$ = 0.14 =
fourteen hundredths

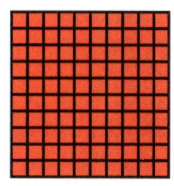

$1\frac{23}{100}$ = 1.23 =
one whole and twenty-three hundredths

Study the examples above. Then, write each fraction as a decimal. Color each balloon with tenths blue. Color each balloon with hundredths green.

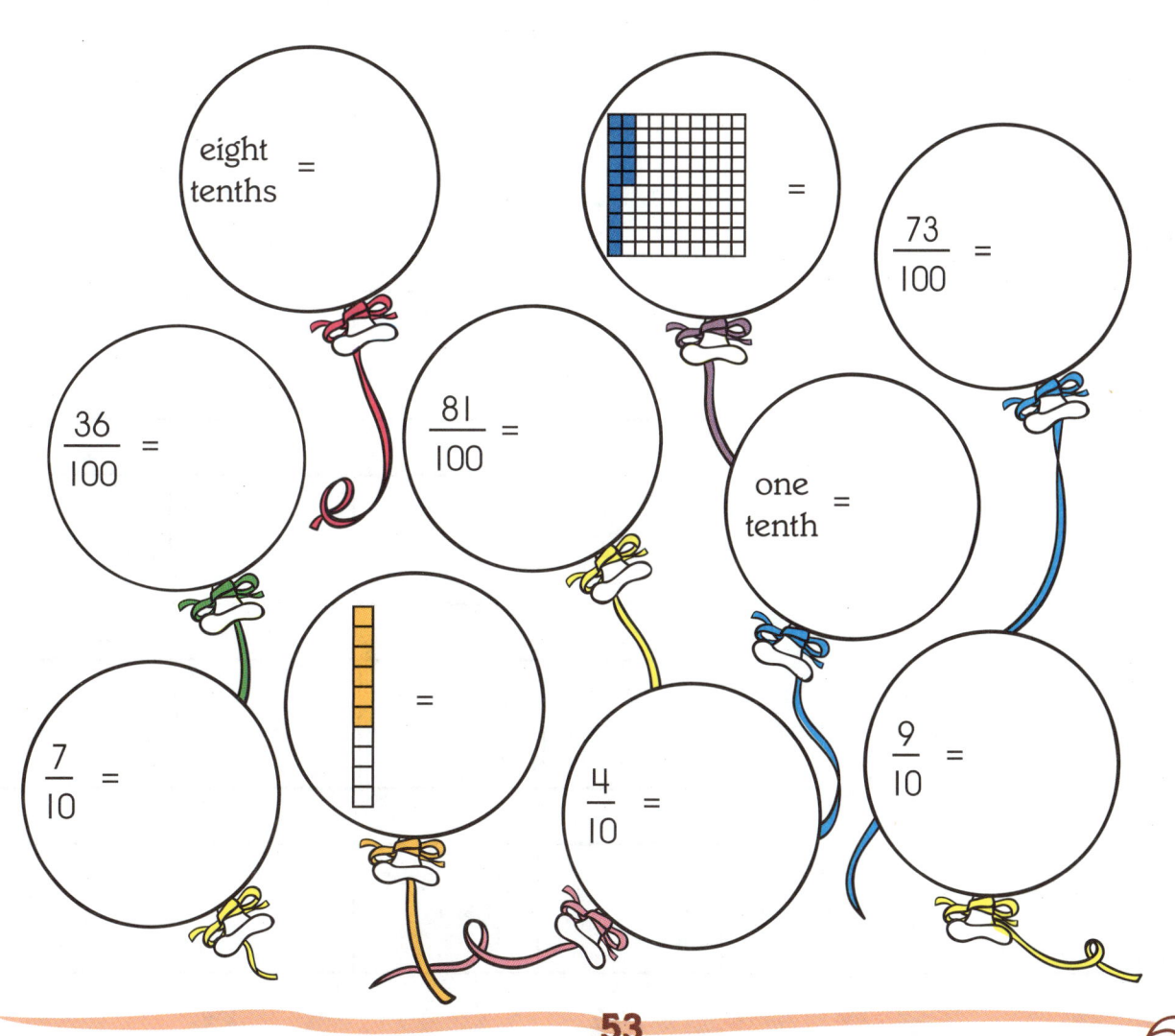

eight tenths =

=

$\frac{73}{100}$ =

$\frac{36}{100}$ =

$\frac{81}{100}$ =

one tenth =

$\frac{7}{10}$ =

=

$\frac{4}{10}$ =

$\frac{9}{10}$ =

Sequencing Decimals

fractions and decimals

To **sequence** decimals with whole numbers, like 1, 2, and 3, treat the numbers as decimals. They are written as 1.0, 2.0, and 3.0. Then, compare the numbers as usual.

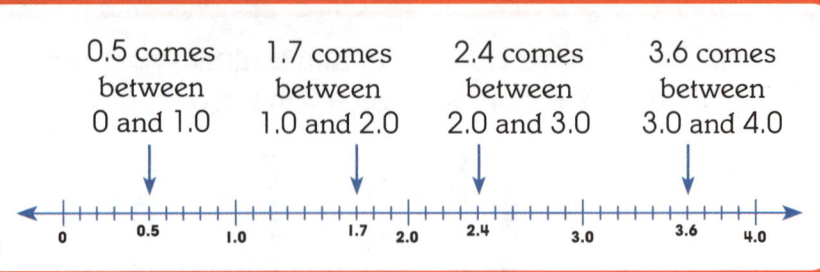

0.5 comes between 0 and 1.0

1.7 comes between 1.0 and 2.0

2.4 comes between 2.0 and 3.0

3.6 comes between 3.0 and 4.0

Study the example above. Then, write the missing numbers.

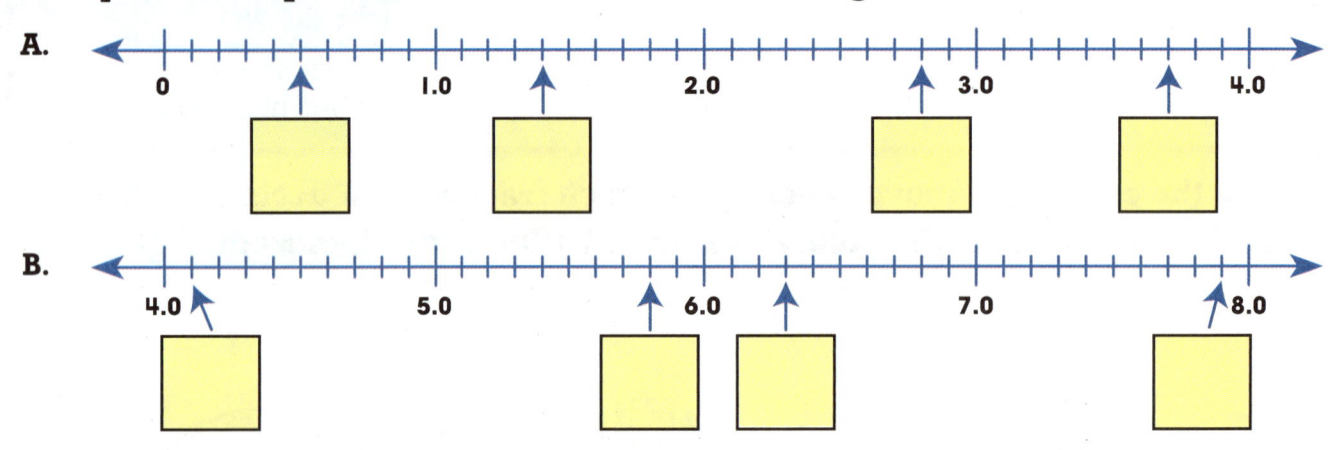

A.

B.

Write the numbers in order from least to greatest. Imagine a number line to help you.

C. 0.1   1.6
   0.7   1.3

D. 2.4   1.9
   0.8   0.3

E. 3.6   2.8
   3.1   0.5

F. 2.6   2.1
   1.4   2.8

Comparing Decimals

fractions and decimals

When comparing decimals, if more of a portion is shaded, this is the greater number.

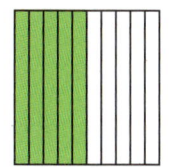

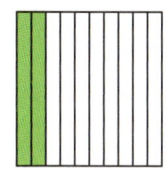

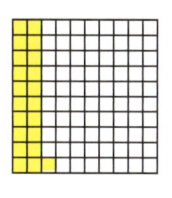

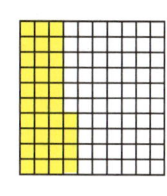

0.5 > 0.2   0.11 < 0.34

Another strategy is to compare the digits in the tenths columns.
0.8 > 0.5
If the digits in the tenths columns are the same, compare the digits in the hundredths columns.
0.63 < 0.69

Compare the decimals using < or >.

A. 0.6 ◯ 0.4   0.1 ◯ 0.5   0.23 ◯ 0.03   0.6 ◯ 0.9

B. 0.06 ◯ 0.60   0.4 ◯ 0.7   0.9 ◯ 0.5   0.7 ◯ 0.6

C. 0.42 ◯ 0.14   0.72 ◯ 0.27   0.25 ◯ 0.52   0.7 ◯ 0.3

D. 1.4 ◯ 1.6   3.5 ◯ 3.7   16.2 ◯ 16.8   5.21 ◯ 5.38

E. 2.48 ◯ 2.35   14.5 ◯ 14.3   42.6 ◯ 42.3   3.8 ◯ 3.9

F. 0.5 ◯ 0.9   0.4 ◯ 0.26   0.8 ◯ 0.7   0.12 ◯ 0.16

G. 0.1 ◯ 0.01   11.3 ◯ 11.5   0.12 ◯ 2.1   13 ◯ 0.13

H. 0.7 ◯ 0.07   0.6 ◯ 0.4   0.2 ◯ 0.1   0.7 ◯ 0.5

Rounding Decimals

fractions and decimals

To **round** decimals:
1. Find the place value you want to round to, and look at the digit just to the right of it.
2. If that digit is less than 5, the number you are rounding stays the same.
3. If that digit is greater than or equal to 5, round the number up.

Example: Round to the nearest tenth.   421.75 = **421.8**

You are rounding to this place. The number to the right tells you whether to round up or down. Since the number is 5, round up.

Study the example above. Then, round to the nearest whole number.

A.	3.67 _____	6.8 _____	11.4 _____	5.9 _____
B.	21.24 _____	10.51 _____	4.9 _____	14.2 _____
C.	8.6 _____	7.8 _____	9.21 _____	10.9 _____
D.	9.7 _____	10.3 _____	8.3 _____	7.4 _____
E.	2.41 _____	12.9 _____	1.02 _____	4.55 _____

Round to the nearest tenth.

F.	6.29 _____	10.68 _____	14.83 _____	6.84 _____
G.	3.48 _____	24.37 _____	17.47 _____	28.15 _____
H.	5.49 _____	10.43 _____	3.56 _____	6.26 _____
I.	17.64 _____	112.26 _____	9.42 _____	400.67 _____
J.	18.25 _____	320.78 _____	62.01 _____	78.45 _____

Summer Bridge Math RB-904088   © Rainbow Bridge Publishing

Adding Decimals

fractions and decimals

1. Line up the decimal points. Write the decimal point in the answer.

```
  3.42
+ 4.89
```

2. Add.

```
  1 1
  3.42
+ 4.89
  8.31
```

Study the example above. Then, solve each problem. Complete the puzzle.

Across:

A. 17.21
  + 8.42

B. 7.64
  + 3.91

C. 3.9
  + 0.8

D. 7.6
  + 2.9

E. 3.41
  + 1.89

F. 0.61
  + 0.49

G. 7.92
  + 0.42

H. 1.3
  + 0.9

Down:

A. 17.24
  + 8.09

C. 3.04
  + 0.99

D. 0.42
  + 0.59

I. 60.42
  + 8.19

J. 3.64
  + 1.95

K. 6.58
  + 0.94

L. 0.81
  + 0.92

M. 25.14
  + 2.98

N. 31.42
  + 9.81

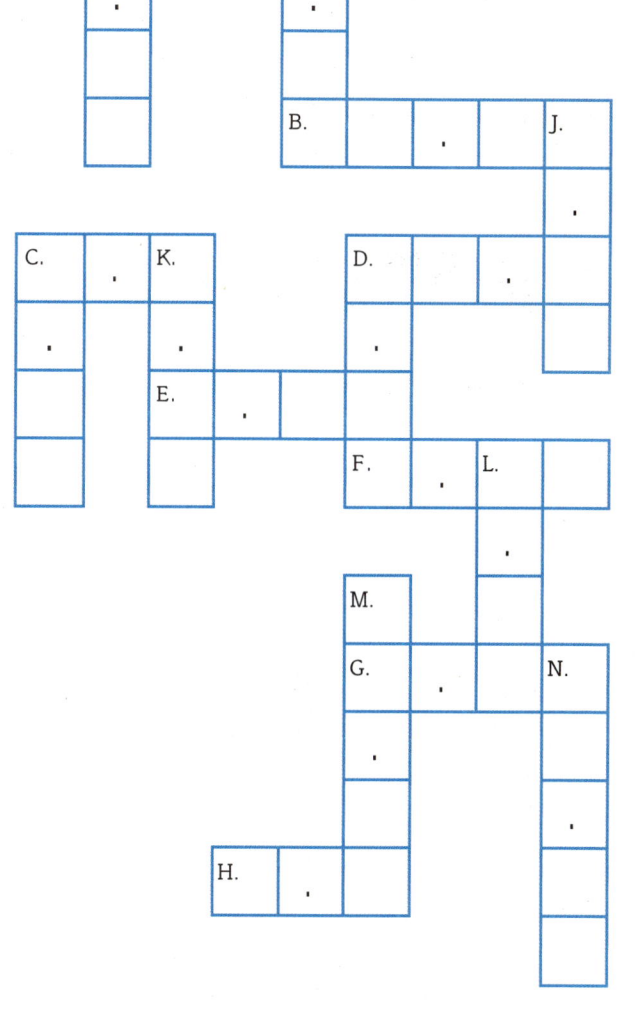

57

Subtracting Decimals

fractions and decimals

1. Line up the decimal points. Place a decimal point in the answer. $\begin{array}{r}23.4\\-8.5\\\hline\end{array}$	2. Subtract. $\begin{array}{r}^{112}\\2\cancel{3}.4\\-8.5\\\hline 14.9\end{array}$

Study the example above. Then, solve each problem. Complete the puzzle.

Across:

A. $\begin{array}{r}14.6\\-2.9\end{array}$
B. $\begin{array}{r}0.6\\-0.2\end{array}$
C. $\begin{array}{r}6.8\\-2.9\end{array}$
D. $\begin{array}{r}5.6\\-2.8\end{array}$
E. $\begin{array}{r}30.4\\-8.2\end{array}$

F. $\begin{array}{r}21.42\\-18.29\end{array}$
G. $\begin{array}{r}5.84\\-1.38\end{array}$
H. $\begin{array}{r}6.5\\-0.9\end{array}$
I. $\begin{array}{r}3.6\\-1.9\end{array}$
J. $\begin{array}{r}2.8\\-1.9\end{array}$

M. $\begin{array}{r}9.42\\-0.09\end{array}$
N. $\begin{array}{r}9.8\\-1.6\end{array}$
O. $\begin{array}{r}4.29\\-1.82\end{array}$
P. $\begin{array}{r}3.42\\-1.89\end{array}$

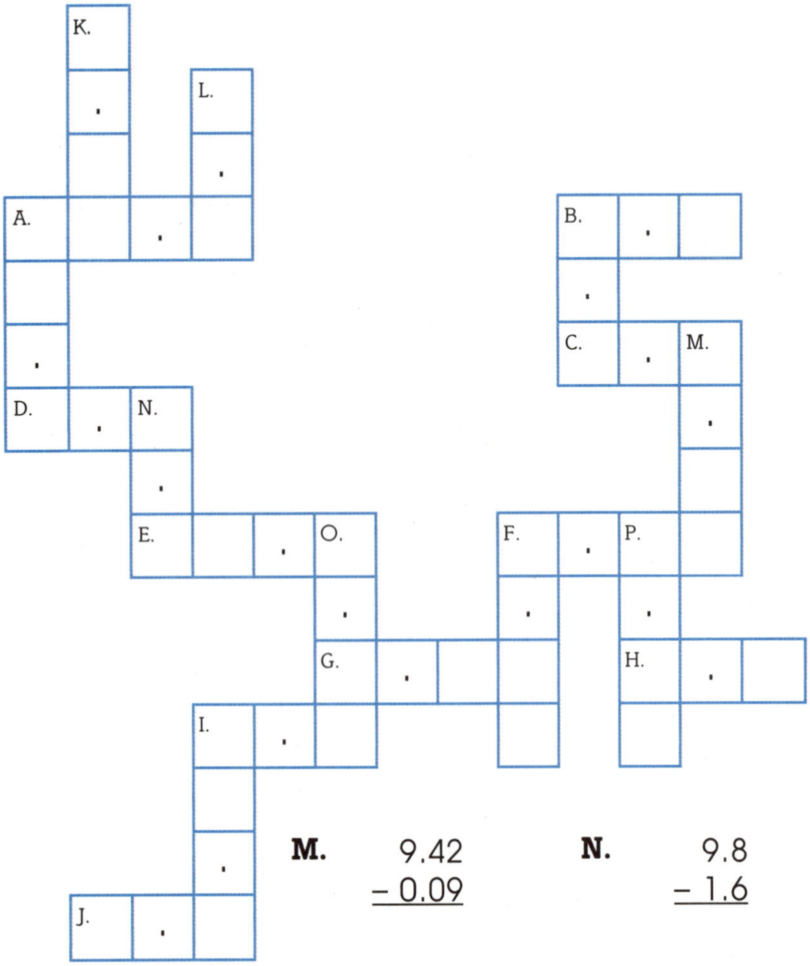

Down:

A. $\begin{array}{r}23.4\\-8.2\end{array}$
B. $\begin{array}{r}0.7\\-0.4\end{array}$

F. $\begin{array}{r}5.42\\-1.79\end{array}$
I. $\begin{array}{r}13.2\\-2.3\end{array}$

K. $\begin{array}{r}3.42\\-1.81\end{array}$
L. $\begin{array}{r}3.9\\-1.2\end{array}$

58

Summer Bridge Math RB-904088 © Rainbow Bridge Publishing

Decimals with Different Place Values
fractions and decimals

| 1. Add a decimal point and 0 where regrouping is needed. Place a decimal point in the answer. $\quad\begin{array}{r}9.00\\-7.76\\\hline.\end{array}$ | 2. Regroup. $\quad\begin{array}{r}{\scriptstyle 8\ 9}\\{\scriptstyle 1\ 1}\\\cancel{9}.\cancel{0}0\\-7.76\\\hline.\end{array}$ | 3. Subtract. $\quad\begin{array}{r}{\scriptstyle 8\ 9}\\{\scriptstyle 1\ 1}\\\cancel{9}.\cancel{0}0\\-7.76\\\hline 1.24\end{array}$ |

Study the example above. Then, solve each problem.

A.
$\begin{array}{r}6\\-3.7\\\hline\end{array}$ $\quad$ $\begin{array}{r}3\\-1.8\\\hline\end{array}$ $\quad$ $\begin{array}{r}2.1\\-1.46\\\hline\end{array}$ $\quad$ $\begin{array}{r}9\\-2.8\\\hline\end{array}$ $\quad$ $\begin{array}{r}4\\-1.6\\\hline\end{array}$

B.
$\begin{array}{r}8\\-2.4\\\hline\end{array}$ $\quad$ $\begin{array}{r}5\\-1.82\\\hline\end{array}$ $\quad$ $\begin{array}{r}6.2\\-3.46\\\hline\end{array}$ $\quad$ $\begin{array}{r}3.5\\-2.67\\\hline\end{array}$ $\quad$ $\begin{array}{r}9.6\\-2\\\hline\end{array}$

C.
$\begin{array}{r}7.3\\-4.28\\\hline\end{array}$ $\quad$ $\begin{array}{r}6\\-2.13\\\hline\end{array}$ $\quad$ $\begin{array}{r}27\\-13.84\\\hline\end{array}$ $\quad$ $\begin{array}{r}7.3\\-2.84\\\hline\end{array}$ $\quad$ $\begin{array}{r}4\\-2.9\\\hline\end{array}$

D.
$\begin{array}{r}5\\-1.64\\\hline\end{array}$ $\quad$ $\begin{array}{r}8.97\\-5.6\\\hline\end{array}$ $\quad$ $\begin{array}{r}8\\-3.64\\\hline\end{array}$ $\quad$ $\begin{array}{r}12\\-4.8\\\hline\end{array}$ $\quad$ $\begin{array}{r}24.8\\-3.94\\\hline\end{array}$

E.
$\begin{array}{r}3\\-2.4\\\hline\end{array}$ $\quad$ $\begin{array}{r}3.4\\-.35\\\hline\end{array}$ $\quad$ $\begin{array}{r}6.1\\-2.56\\\hline\end{array}$ $\quad$ $\begin{array}{r}8\\-.25\\\hline\end{array}$ $\quad$ $\begin{array}{r}25.4\\-14.28\\\hline\end{array}$

Tenths
fractions and decimals

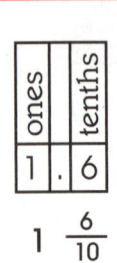

ones	tenths
1 .	6

$1\frac{6}{10}$

What portion of this box is shaded?
one whole box

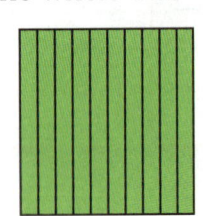

What portion of this box is shaded?
six tenths of the box

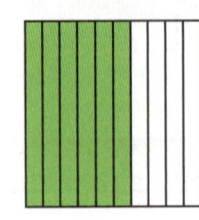

Altogether: 1.6 (one and six tenths)
Or, "One point six," or "one and six tenths."

$\underline{\quad 1 . 6 \quad}$
one . six tenths

Example:

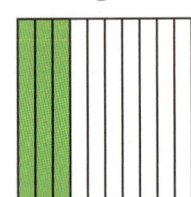

Fraction: $\frac{3}{10}$

Decimal: 0.3

When there are no whole numbers, place a "0" in the ones place, just to the left of the decimal point.

$\underline{\quad 0 . 3 \quad}$
no ones . three tenths

Study the examples above. Then, write as both a fraction and a decimal.

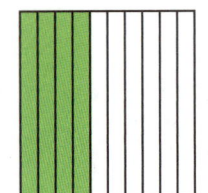

A. Fraction: _____
   Decimal: _____

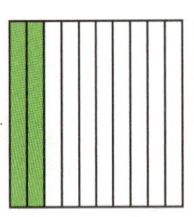

B. Fraction: _____
   Decimal: _____

C. Fraction: _____
   Decimal: _____

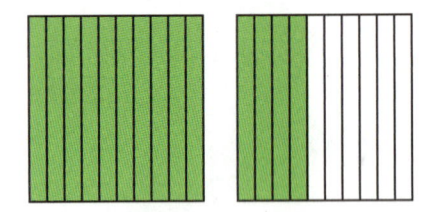

D. Fraction: _____
   Decimal: _____

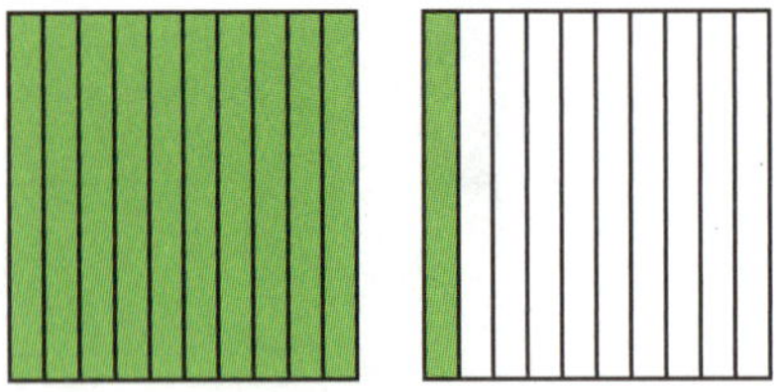

E. Fraction: _____
   Decimal: _____

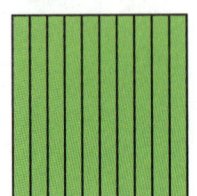

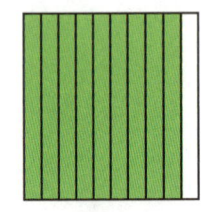

F. Fraction: _____
   Decimal: _____

Summer Bridge Math RB-904088 © Rainbow Bridge Publishing

Hundredths

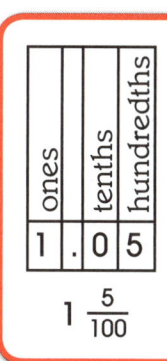

fractions and decimals

ones	tenths	hundredths
1	. 0	5

$1\frac{5}{100}$

What portion of this box is shaded?
one whole box

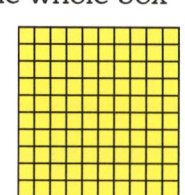

What portion of this box is shaded?
five hundredths of a box

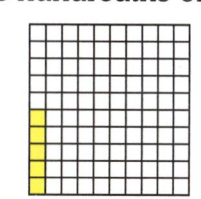

Altogether: 1.05
(one and five hundredths)

$\dfrac{1.05}{\text{one . no tenths five hundredths}}$

Study the examples above. Then, write as both a fraction and a decimal.

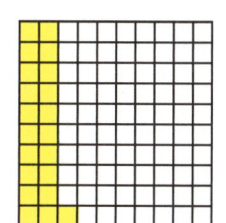

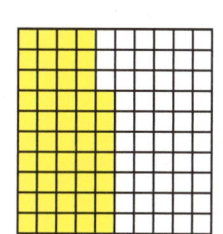

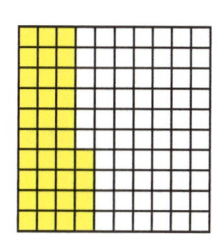

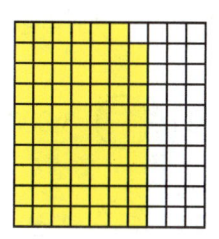

A. Fraction: _____
Decimal: _____

B. Fraction: _____
Decimal: _____

C. Fraction: _____
Decimal: _____

D. Fraction: _____
Decimal: _____

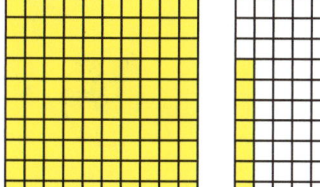

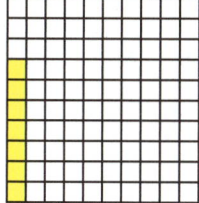

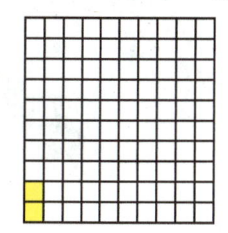

E. Fraction: _____
Decimal: _____

F. Fraction: _____
Decimal: _____

G. Fraction: _____
Decimal: _____

H. Fraction: _____
Decimal: _____

Capacity and Weight in the Standard System

measurement

2 cups (c.) = 1 pint (pt.)
2 pints = 1 quart (qt.)
4 quarts = 1 gallon (gal.)
16 ounces (oz.) = 1 pound (lb.)
2,000 pounds = 1 ton (t.)

1 oz.    1 lb.    1 t.

Study the units of measurement above. Then, compare using >, <, or =.

A. 14 oz. ◯ 1 lb.   4 c. ◯ 1 pt.   2 qt. ◯ 2 pt.

B. 3 gal. ◯ 12 qt.   1 qt. ◯ 3 pt.   3 lb. ◯ 32 oz.

C. 2 t. ◯ 3,000 lb.   4 c. ◯ 2 pt.   1 t. ◯ 2,000 lb.

D. 2 c. ◯ 2 pt.   3 qt. ◯ 1 gal.   2 lb. ◯ 30 oz.

E. 8 qt. ◯ 3 gal.   17 oz. ◯ 1 lb.   1 qt. ◯ 4 pt.

Circle the most appropriate unit of measurement.

F.
oz.   lb.    lb.   t.    c.   gal.    oz.   lb. 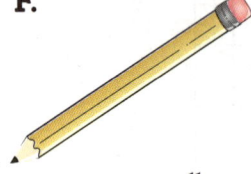

G.
c.   qt.    pt.   gal.    oz.   lb.    c.   gal. 

Convert each unit.

H. 3 lb. = _____ oz.   2 t. = _____ lb.   2 gal. = _____ qt.

I. 2 qt. = _____ pt.   3 pt. = _____ c.   3 qt. = _____ pt.

J. 5 lb. = _____ oz.   5 qt. = _____ pt.   8 gal. = _____ qt.

Capacity in the Metric System

measurement

A **milliliter** (mL) is used to measure the capacity of very small amounts.
A **liter** (L) is used to measure the capacity of large amounts.

1 mL   1 L

1 L = 1,000 mL
To change liters to milliliters, multiply by 1,000. To change milliliters to liters, divide by 1,000.

Since 1 L = 1,000 mL,
7 L = 7,000 mL

Study the example above. Then, find each missing number.

A. 5 L = _____ mL   3 L = _____ mL   8 L = _____ mL   1 L = _____ mL

B. 7 L = _____ mL   9 L = _____ mL   2 L = _____ mL   11 L = _____ mL

Circle the best estimate for the capacity of each item.

C. 
500 mL   500 L    1,000 mL   1,000 L    20 mL   20 L

D. 
15 mL   15 L 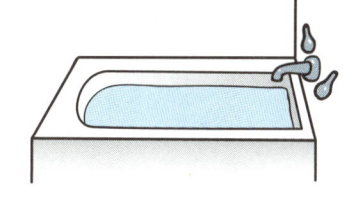   120 mL   120 L    4 mL   4 L

E. 
5 mL   5 L    80,000 mL   80,000 L    400 mL   400 L

F. 
255 mL   255 L    17 mL   17 L    10 mL   10 L

Weight in the Metric System

measurement

A **gram** is a metric unit used to measure the weight of light objects, such as a piece of paper or a spoonful of sugar.

A **kilogram** is used to weigh heavy objects like people or trucks.

1 gram (g)

1 kilogram (kg) = 1,000 grams (g)
To change kilograms to grams, multiply by 1,000. To change grams to kilograms, divide by 1,000.

Since 1 kg = 1,000 g,
5 kg = 5,000 g.

1 kilogram (kg)

Study the examples above. Then, circle the correct unit of measurement.

A.

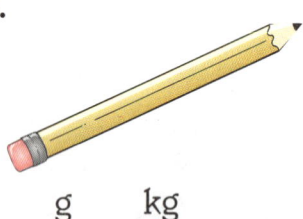

pencil — g   kg
computer — g   kg
apple — g   kg
bow — g   kg

B.

bench — g   kg
eraser — g   kg 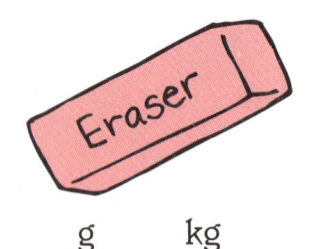 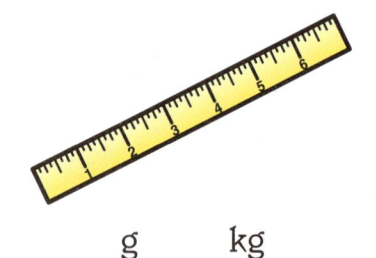
ruler — g   kg

Circle the best estimate for the mass of each item.

C.

girl — 60 g   60 kg 
popcorn — 11 g   11 kg 
chicken — 1 g   1 kg

D.

muffin — 15 g   15 kg 
glasses — 30 g   30 kg 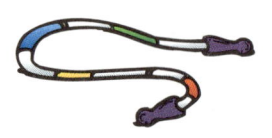
jump rope — 10 g   10 kg 
backpack — 7 g   7 kg

64

Summer Bridge Math RB-904088 © Rainbow Bridge Publishing

Length in the Standard System

measurement

12 inches (in.) = 1 foot (ft.)
3 feet (ft.) = 1 yard (yd.)
5,280 feet (ft.) = 1 mile (mi.)
1,760 yards (yd.) = 1 mile (mi.)

1 in.
1 ft.
1 yd.
1 mi.

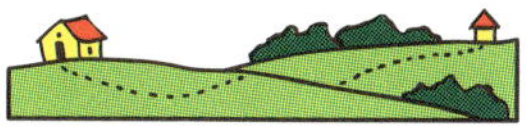

Measure the length of each line to the nearest inch or half-inch.

A. _____ in.
B. _____ in.
C. _____ in.
D. _____ in.
E. _____ in.
F. _____ in.

Study the equivalents above. Then, find each missing number.

G. 3 ft. = _____ in.   3 yd. = _____ ft.   2 mi. = _____ yd.

H. 10 ft. = _____ in.   4 mi. = _____ ft.   5 yd. = _____ ft.

I. 8 ft. = _____ in.   7 ft. = _____ in.   10 yd. = _____ ft.

J. 1 mi. = _____ ft.   2 yd. = _____ ft.   6 yd. = _____ ft.

Circle the most appropriate unit of measure.

K.

in.   yd.    in.   yd.    in.   mi. 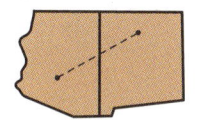   yd.   mi.

L.

mi.   yd.    ft.   yd.    in.   ft.    yd.   mi.

Length in the Metric System

measurement

100 centimeters = 1 meter
1,000 meters = 1 kilometer
100 cm = 1 m
1,000 m = 1 km

1 centimeter (cm)   1 meter (m)   1 kilometer (km)

Study the units of measurement above. Then, choose the best unit to measure each.

A.	The length of your car.	cm	m	km
B.	The distance from your house to school.	cm	m	km
C.	The length of your pencil.	cm	m	km
D.	The distance from your house to a grocery store.	cm	m	km
E.	The distance from your city to Washington, D.C.	cm	m	km
F.	The length of a swimming pool.	cm	m	km
G.	The length of your pinky finger.	cm	m	km
H.	The height of a tree.	cm	m	km
I.	The width of a quarter.	cm	m	km
J.	The width of this book.	cm	m	km

Find each missing number.

K. 8 km = _____ m   4 km = _____ m

L. 10 km = _____ m   6 km = _____ m

M. 5 m = _____ cm   70 m = _____ cm

N. 2 km = _____ m   9 km = _____ m

O. 7 m = _____ cm   100 km = _____ m

Pictographs and Bar Graphs

charts and graphs

Pictographs use pictures to compare information.

Each ⭐ stands for 2 awards.

Good Deed Awards
Mark ⭐⭐⭐⭐
Gwen ⭐⭐⭐⭐⭐
Emily ⭐⭐⭐
Katie ⭐
Billy ⭐⭐⭐

Bar graphs use bars to compare information.

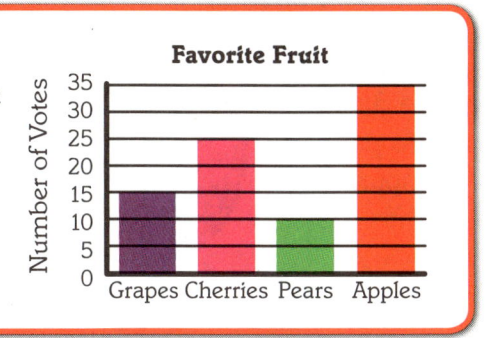

Favorite Fruit

Use the graphs to answer each question.

Lindy Elementary Food Drive

Each 🥫 stands for 100 lb. of donated food.

A. Which grade level had the most donations? _____

B. Which grade level had only 200 pounds of food donated? _____

C. What was the total amount of food donated for the entire school? _____

D. How much more did fourth grade donate than fifth grade? _____

E. Who donated more, first or sixth grade? _____

F. How many more pounds did kindergarten donate than fifth grade? _____

G. Which grade level donated a total of 500 pounds? _____

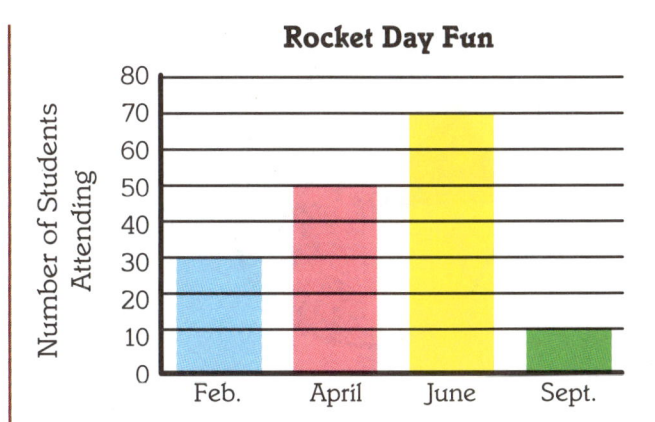

Rocket Day Fun

H. Which month had the greatest attendance at Rocket Day? _____

I. How many more students attended Rocket Day in Feb. than in Sept.? _____

J. Which month had 50 students attend? _____

K. How many more students attended in June than in April? _____

L. What was the total number of students that attended in all? _____

M. Which month had the least number of students attending? _____

N. How many less students attended in Sept. than in June? _____

Circle Graphs and Line Graphs

charts and graphs

Circle graphs are divided into parts to display facts.

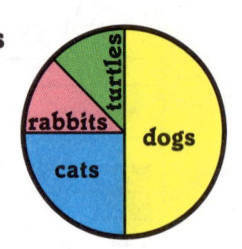

Line graphs are used to show change.

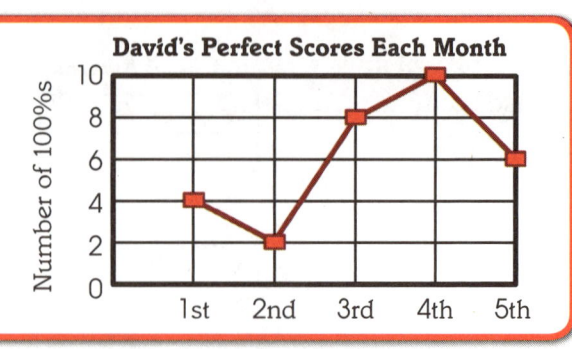

Use the graphs to answer each question.

Favorite Vegetables

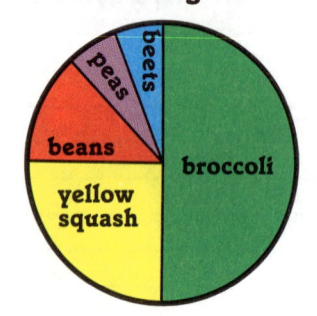

Eva's Babysitting Jobs

A. Which two vegetables are the least favorite? _____

B. Which is the favorite vegetable? _____

C. Which vegetable is liked half as much as broccoli? _____

D. Which vegetable is liked more, peas or beans? _____

E. Which vegetable is liked twice as much as yellow squash? _____

F. Which vegetable is liked twice as much as beans? _____

G. Which vegetable is as popular as all the other vegetables combined? _____

H. Which month was Eva called for the most babysitting jobs? _____

I. Between which two months was the greatest decrease in calls to babysit? ____

J. Between which two months was the greatest increase in babysitting jobs? ____

K. What was the total number of babysitting jobs from October through December? _____

L. Which two months tied for the least number of babysitting jobs? _____

M. What was the total number of babysitting jobs for the months displayed? _____

Points on a Grid

charts and graphs

The **ordered pair** tells where the point is on this grid. (over 2, up 3)

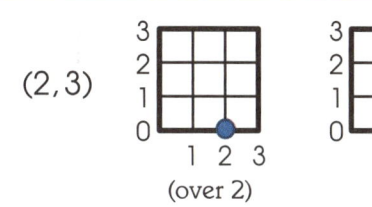

The first number tells how many **units** the point is to the right of the zero. (over 2)
The second number tells how many units to go up. (up 3)

Study the examples above. Then, write each ordered pair.

A. A = (___, ___)   B = (___, ___)

B. C = (___, ___)   D = (___, ___)

C. E = (___, ___)   F = (___, ___)

D. G = (___, ___)   H = (___, ___)

E. I = (___, ___)   J = (___, ___)

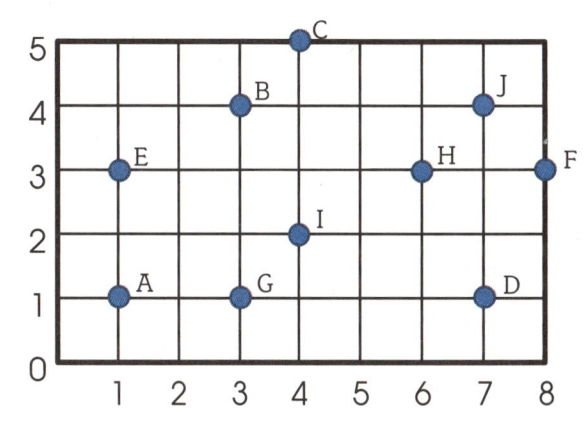

Write each ordered pair. What is the secret message?

F. (4, 6) ___   (1, 1) ___   (6, 2) ___   (5, 1) ___

G. (7, 7) ___   (1, 1) ___   (4, 3) ___   (1, 1) ___

H. (5, 1) ___   (1, 4) ___   (0, 5) ___   (1, 4) ___

I. (8, 3) ___   (4, 3) ___

J. (2, 7) ___   (2, 7) ___

K. (6, 5) ___   (2, 4) ___

L. (3, 2) ___   (8, 1) ___

M. (1, 4) ___   (5, 1) ___

N. (5, 1) ___   (7, 4) ___

69

© Rainbow Bridge Publishing   Summer Bridge Math RB-904088

Using a Thermometer

charts and graphs

Degrees **Fahrenheit** (°F)	Degrees **Celsius** (°C)
212° → water boils 98.6° → normal body temperature 75° → nice picnic weather 32° → water freezes	100° → water boils 37° → normal body temperature 24° → nice picnic weather 0° → water freezes

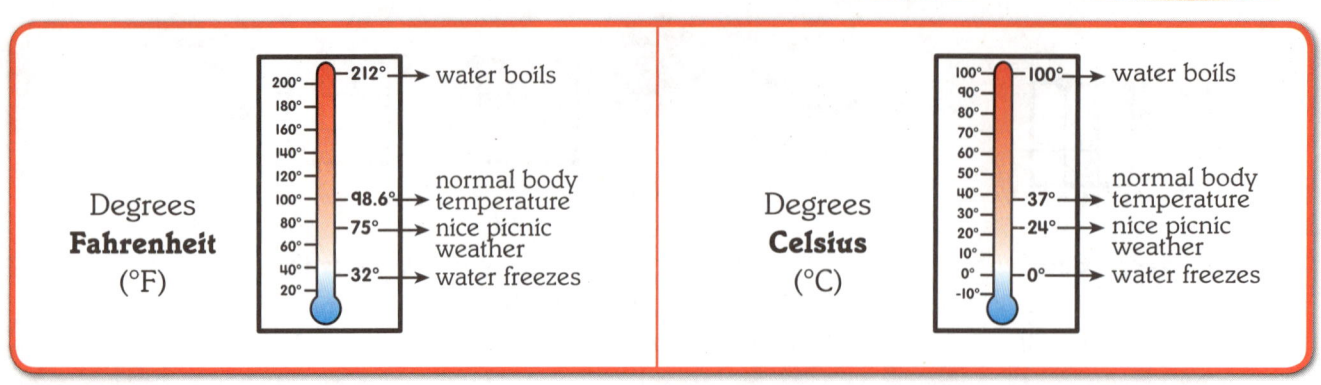

Study the thermometers above. Then, write each temperature.

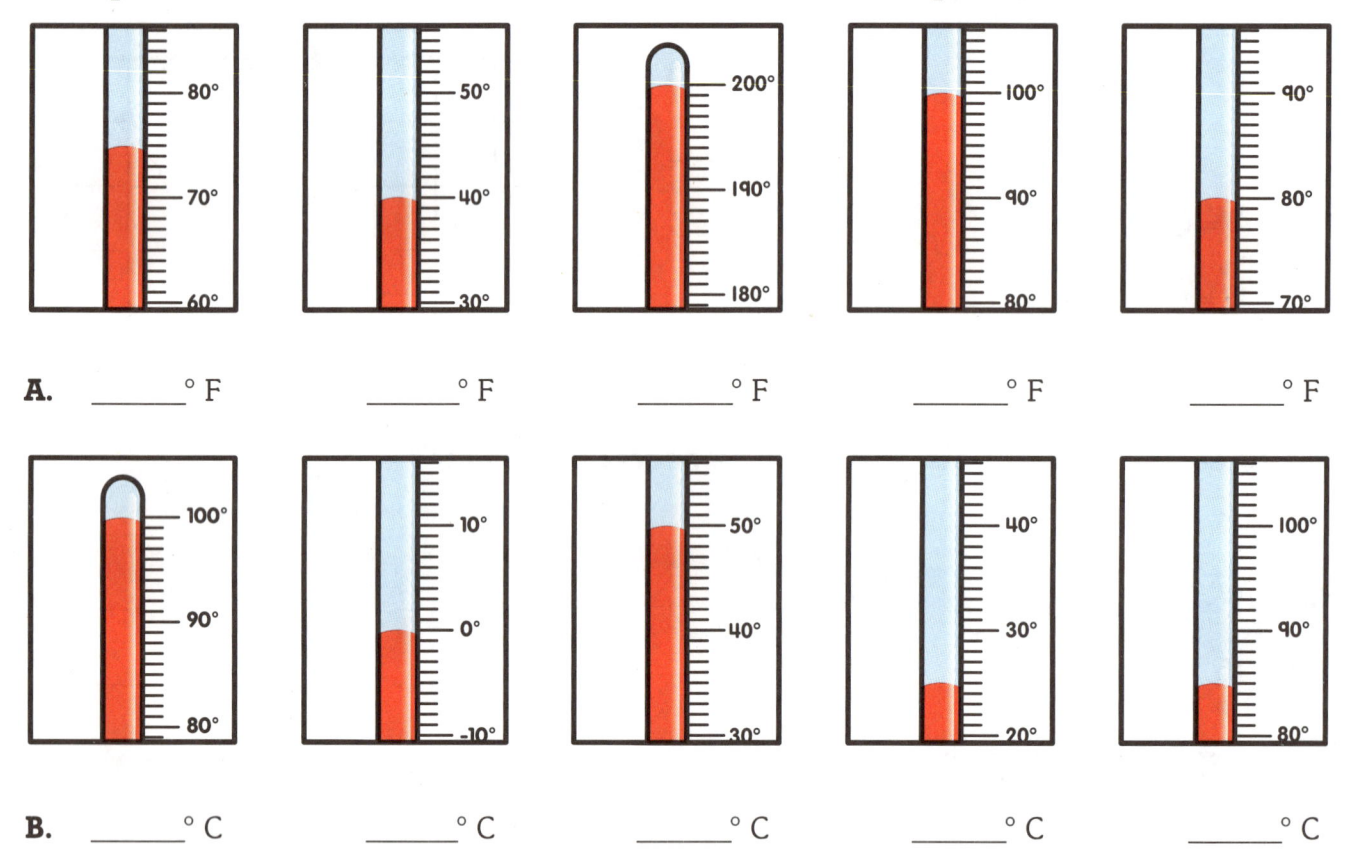

A. _____ °F   _____ °F   _____ °F   _____ °F   _____ °F

B. _____ °C   _____ °C   _____ °C   _____ °C   _____ °C

Match the temperatures (°C and °F).

C. Playing in the snow _____ _____
D. Water boiling _____ _____
E. Normal body temperature _____ _____
F. A nice day for a picnic _____ _____
G. Water freezing _____ _____

a. 32°F   f. 100°C
b. 98.6°F   g. 75°F
c. 212°F   h. 0°C
d. 37°C   i. 24°C
e. 28°F   j. -2°C

Using a Calendar

charts and graphs

There are 7 **days** in a **week**. Sunday is the first day of the week. There are 52 weeks in a year. There are 12 **months** in a **year**. There are $365\frac{1}{4}$ days in a year. $\frac{1}{4} + \frac{1}{4} + \frac{1}{4} + \frac{1}{4} = 1$ extra day—it is added to February during a leap year. Every fourth year, February has 29 days. February has 28 days in non-leap years. April, June, September, and November have 30 days. January, March, May, July, August, October, and December have 31 days.

Answer each question using the calendar for March.

A. The first of March is on what day? _____

B. What date in March is the first Sunday? _____

C. How many full weeks are there in March? _____

D. What day is 7 days after Monday, March 12? _____

E. What day does the last day in March fall on? _____
   What is the date? _____

F. What day does March 22 fall on? _____

G. What is the date for the last Tuesday in March? _____

March
S M T W Th F S
1 2 3
4 5 6 7 8 9 10
11 12 13 14 15 16 17
18 19 20 21 22 23 24
25 26 27 28 29 30 31

Answer each question using the calendar for July.

H. What day does July 4 fall on? _____

I. What day does July 20 fall on? _____

J. What date does the last Tuesday in July fall on? _____

K. Thursday, the 19th of July, is how many weeks past the 5 of July? _____

L. What is the date of the third Sunday in July? _____

M. What day comes 4 days after Saturday, July 21? _____

N. What is the date on the second Saturday in July? _____

July
S M T W Th F S
1 2 3 4 5 6 7
8 9 10 11 12 13 14
15 16 17 18 19 20 21
22 23 24 25 26 27 28
29 30 31

Symmetry

geometry

If you can fold a figure in half and both sides are identical, it is said to be **symmetrical**.

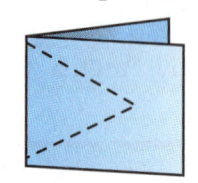

A **line of symmetry** will divide a figure in half. Each side will be identical in shape.

Some figures have many different lines of symmetry.

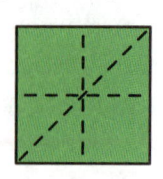

Study the examples above. Then, look at each figure. Is each figure symmetrical? Write yes or no.

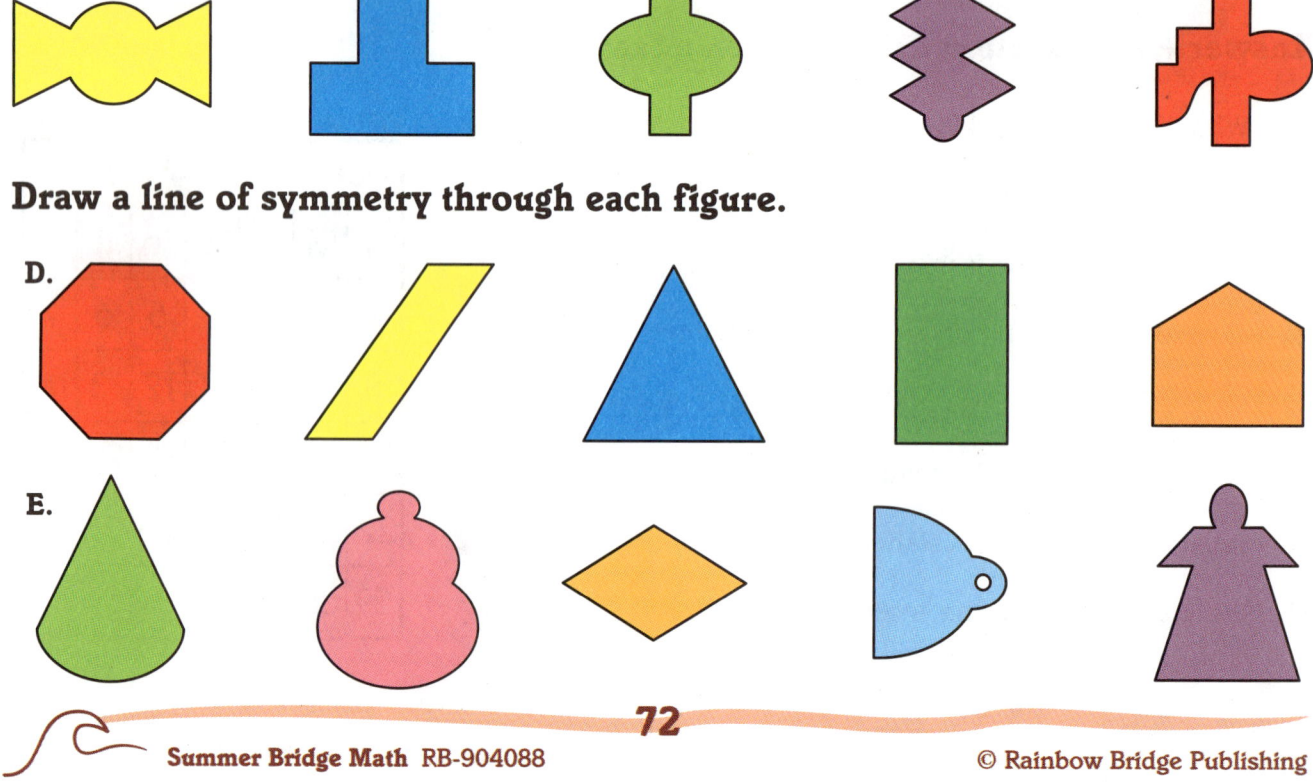

A.

B.

C.

Draw a line of symmetry through each figure.

D.

E.

Shapes

geometry

| **Parallel lines** run side by side and never cross. | A **quadrilateral** is any shape with 4 sides. |

Look at the shapes. Then, answer each question.

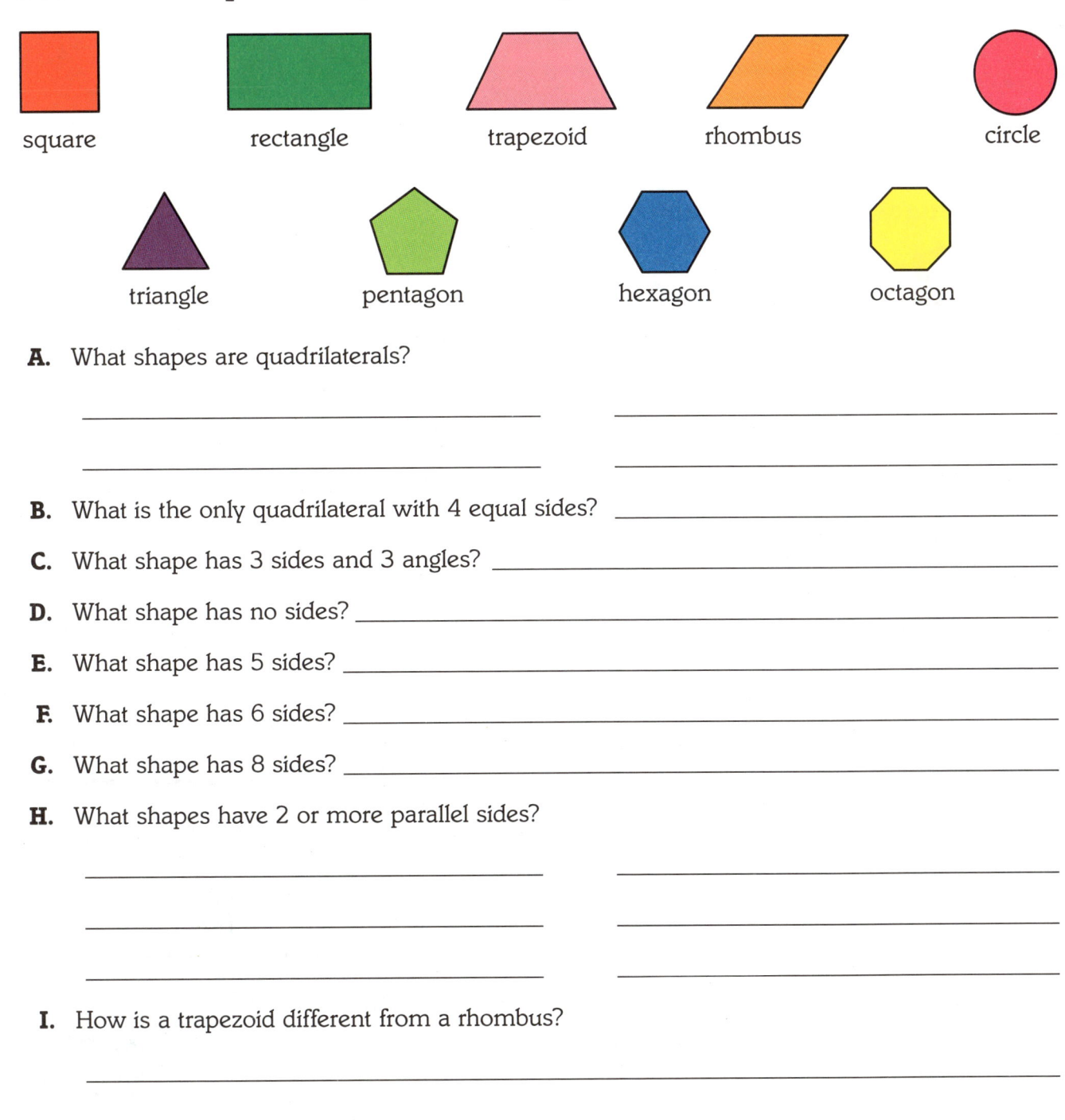

square   rectangle   trapezoid   rhombus   circle

triangle   pentagon   hexagon   octagon

A. What shapes are quadrilaterals?
_____   _____
_____   _____

B. What is the only quadrilateral with 4 equal sides? _____

C. What shape has 3 sides and 3 angles? _____

D. What shape has no sides? _____

E. What shape has 5 sides? _____

F. What shape has 6 sides? _____

G. What shape has 8 sides? _____

H. What shapes have 2 or more parallel sides?
_____   _____
_____   _____
_____   _____

I. How is a trapezoid different from a rhombus?
_____   _____
_____   _____

Polygons

geometry

When 3 or more line segments come together, they form a **polygon**. The points where the line segments meet are called **vertices**.

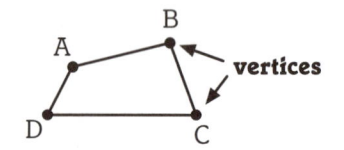

A polygon with 3 sides: 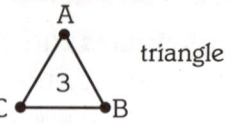 triangle

A polygon with 4 sides: quadrilateral

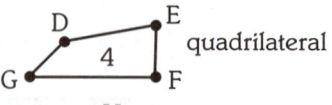

A polygon with 5 sides: 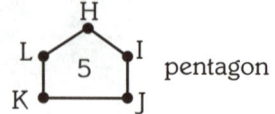 pentagon

Study the examples above. Then, identify each polygon as a triangle, a quadrilateral, or a pentagon.

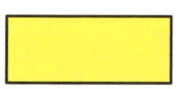

A.

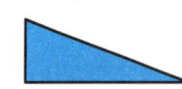

B.

C.

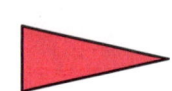

A **parallelogram** is a special type of quadrilateral that has opposite sides that are parallel and the same length.

A **rectangle** is a parallelogram that has 4 right angles.

A **square** is a rectangle with 4 sides equal in length.

Identify each polygon as a parallelogram, a rectangle, or a square.

D.

Similar and Congruent Figures

geometry

> Figures that are the same shape but not the same size are called **similar**. 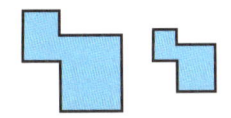
>
> Figures that are the same size and shape are called **congruent**.

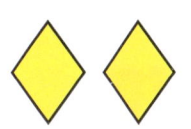

Study the examples above. Then, using a ruler, connect the dots to draw lines to the figures that are similar. Are the 2 figures you made similar? _____

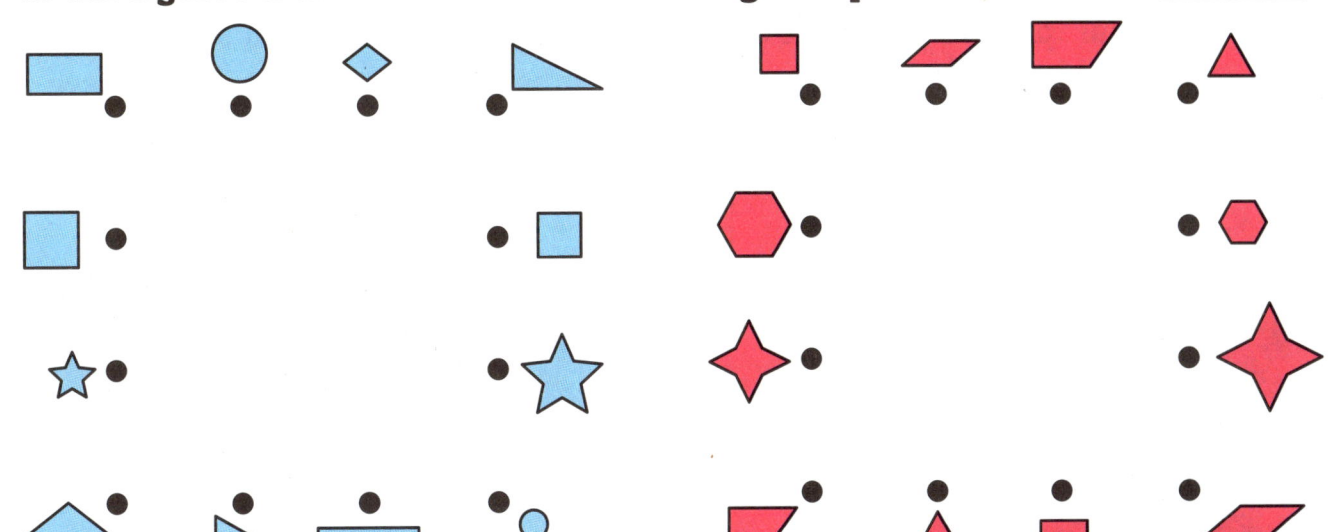

Using a ruler, connect the dots to draw lines to the figures that are congruent. Are the 2 figures you made congruent? _____

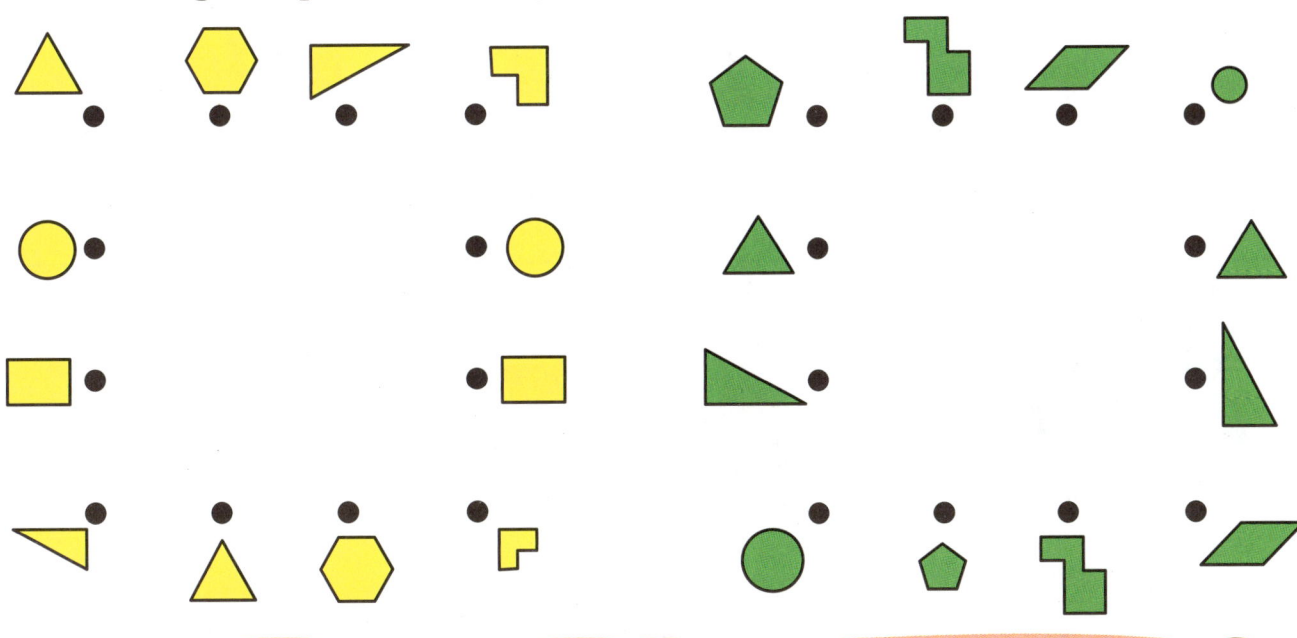

Labeling Congruency and Movements

geometry

Congruent means two shapes are exactly the same in size and shape. The congruent figures may look different because their positions are different. The change in direction is called **movement**, and there are 3 types.

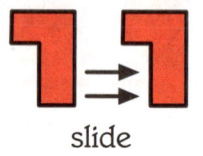

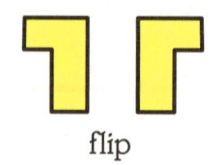

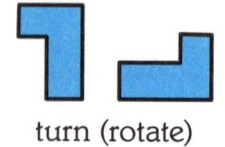

slide   flip   turn (rotate)

Study the examples above and on page 75. Then, decide if each set of shapes is congruent. If they are congruent, label the movement. If they are not congruent, write no.

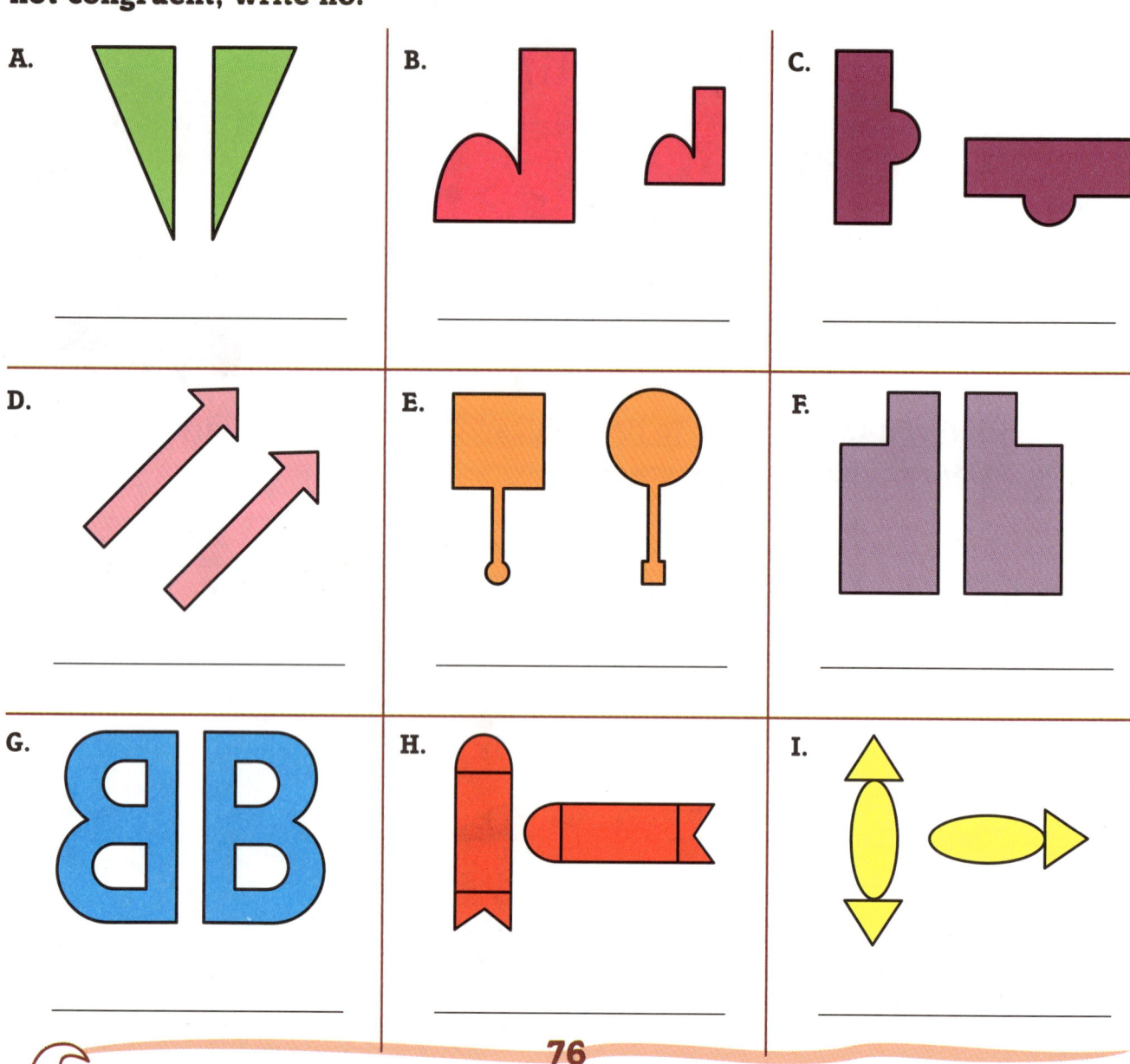

A.

B.

C.

D.

E.

F.

G.

H.

I.

Solid Figures

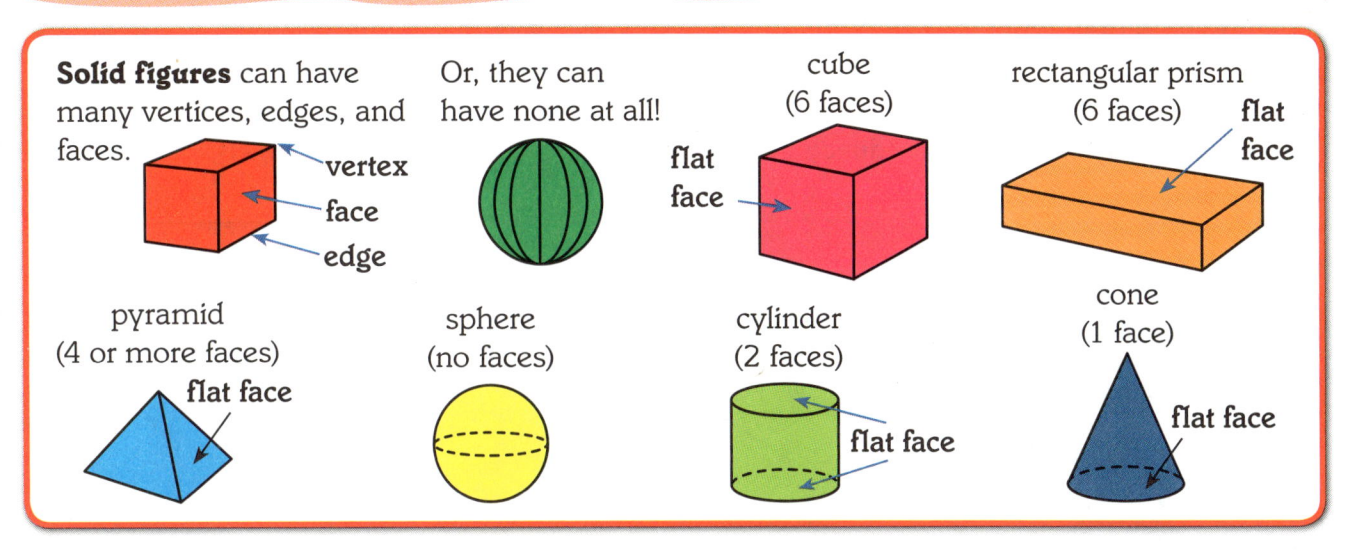

geometry

Solid figures can have many vertices, edges, and faces. — vertex, face, edge

Or, they can have none at all!

cube (6 faces) — flat face

rectangular prism (6 faces) — flat face

pyramid (4 or more faces) — flat face

sphere (no faces)

cylinder (2 faces) — flat face

cone (1 face) — flat face

Study the solid figures above. Then, identify each solid figure.

A.

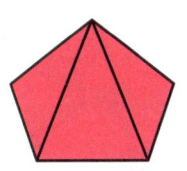

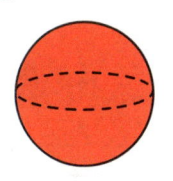

B.

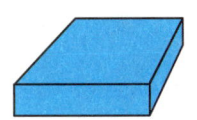

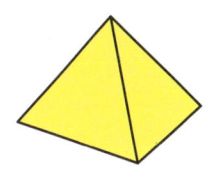

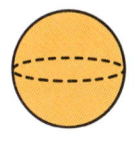

C.

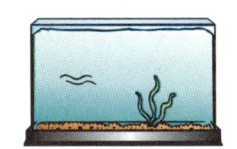

D.

Line Segments, Lines, and Rays

geometry

The straight path between points X and Y is a **line segment**. (segment XY)

A **line** is a straight path that goes unending in two directions. (line CD)

A **ray** is a straight path that begins at a point and goes unending in one direction. (ray TU)

Lines that never meet are called **parallel** lines.

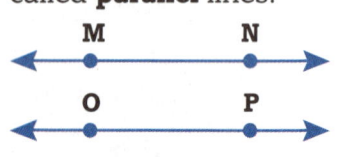

Lines that cross are called **intersecting** lines.

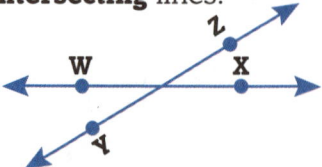

Lines that cross at right angles are called **perpendicular** lines.

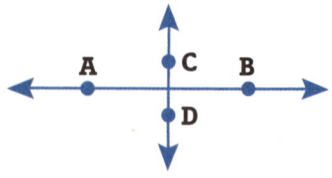

Study the examples above. Then, using the appropriate letters, identify each line segment, line, or ray.

A.

C D   L M   X Y   A B

_____   _____   _____   _____

B.

B C   S T   E F   E D

_____   _____   _____   _____

Identify each as parallel lines, intersecting lines, or perpendicular lines.

C.

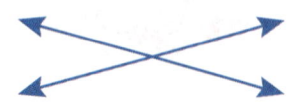

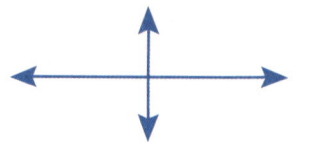

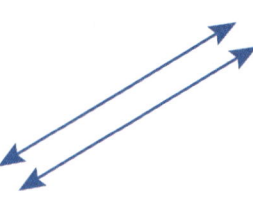

_____   _____   _____   _____

D. Draw 2 parallel lines. Then, draw 2 intersecting lines across the 2 parallel lines.

78

Summer Bridge Math RB-904088   © Rainbow Bridge Publishing

Angles

geometry

> The point at which 2 rays meet to form an angle is called a **vertex**. Point N is the vertex. 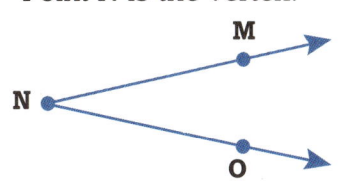
>
> An angle that is less than 90° is called an **acute** angle. 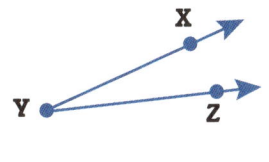
>
> An angle that is 90° is a **right** angle. A square is made up of right angles. 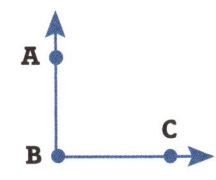
>
> An angle greater than 90° is called an **obtuse** angle.

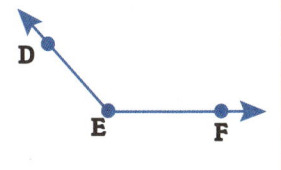

Study the examples above. Then, identify each angle as acute, right, or obtuse.

A.

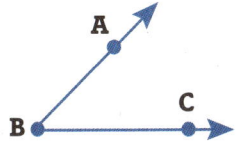

_____ _____ _____

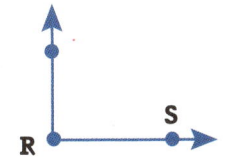

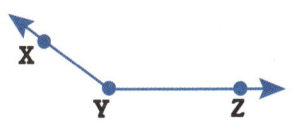

B.

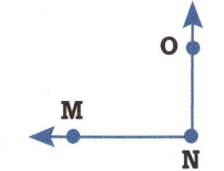

_____ _____ _____

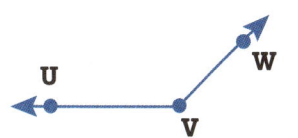

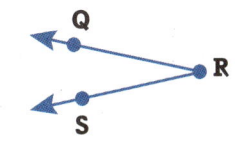

C.

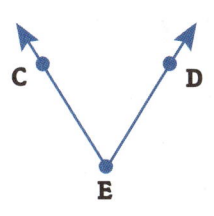

_____ _____ _____

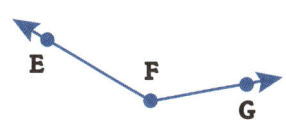

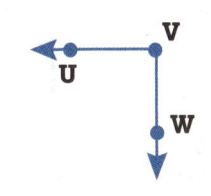

D.

_____

Draw one obtuse angle.
Draw one acute angle.

Identifying Parts of Shapes

geometry

A **square** has 4 sides. It also has 4 line segments, four angles, 4 points, and 2 sets of parallel lines.

endpoint → endpoint → line segment   closed curve   ← angle   parallel lines

Study the examples above. Then, use the pictures to complete the chart.

Shape	Number of Line Segments	Number of Endpoints	Number of Angles	Any Parallel Lines?	Any Closed Curves?
rectangle					
triangle					
trapezoid					
circle					
house shape					
pentagon					
S-curve					

80

Summer Bridge Math RB-904088 © Rainbow Bridge Publishing

Perimeter

geometry

The **perimeter (P)** of a figure is the distance around that figure. The perimeter is measured in units, which may be inches, centimeters, miles, etc. To find the perimeter, add all of the sides together.

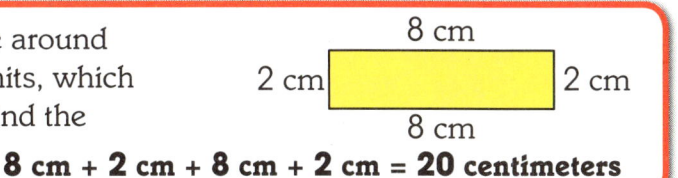

8 cm + 2 cm + 8 cm + 2 cm = **20 centimeters**

Study the example above. Then, find the perimeter of each figure. Label your answer in the units indicated.

A. 8 units (top), 4 units (left), 5 units (right), 7 units (bottom)

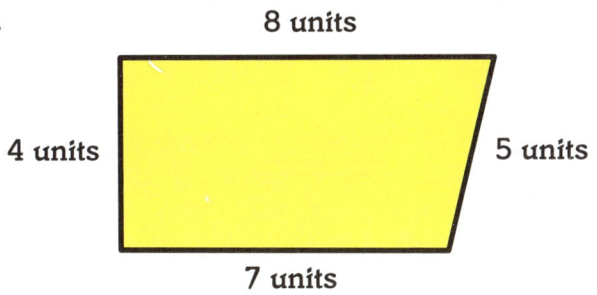

P = _____

B. 2 units (top), 1 unit, 1 unit, 2 units (left), 1 unit, 3 units (bottom)

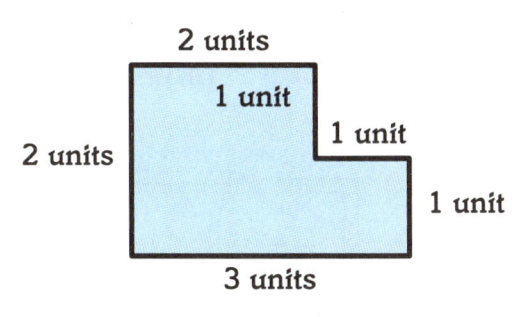

P = _____

C. 8 inches, 6 inches, 10 inches

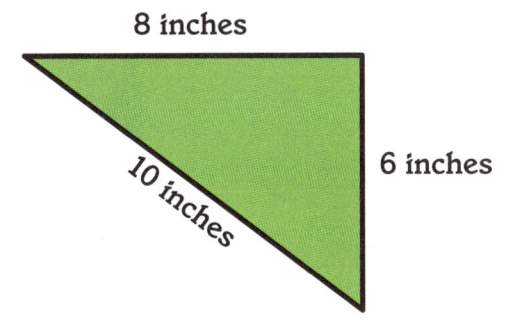

P = _____

D. 4 cm (top), 2 cm, 3 cm, 4 cm (left), 2 cm, 1 cm

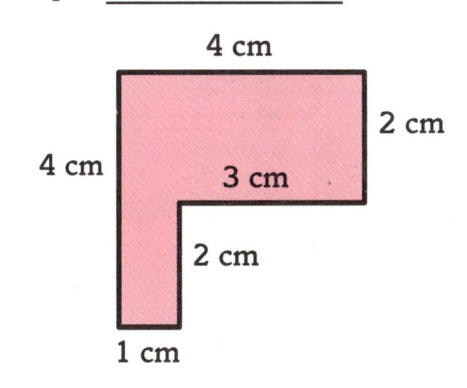

P = _____

E. 7 miles, 7 miles, 7 miles

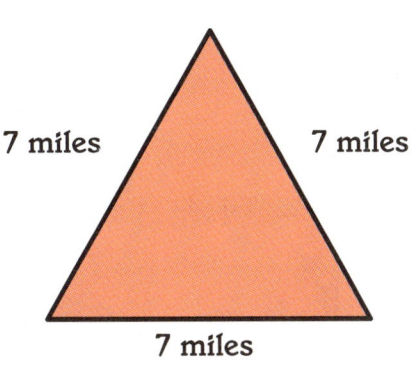

P = _____

F. 8 miles, 2 miles, 2 miles, 3 miles, 3 miles, 6 miles, 6 miles, 2 miles

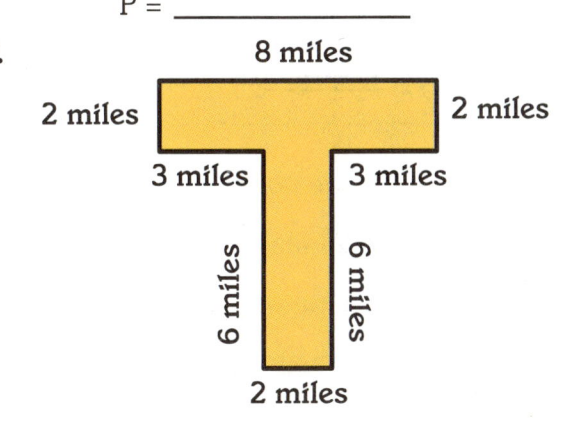

P = _____

Area

geometry

What is the **area** of rectangle A?
Multiply. 5 feet x 30 feet = 150 square feet
What is the area of rectangle B?
Multiply. 8 feet x 10 feet = 80 square feet
How much larger is rectangle A than rectangle B?
Subtract. 150 square feet – 80 square feet = **70 square feet**

Study the example above. Then, use the picture to answer each question about the Wong family's upstairs.

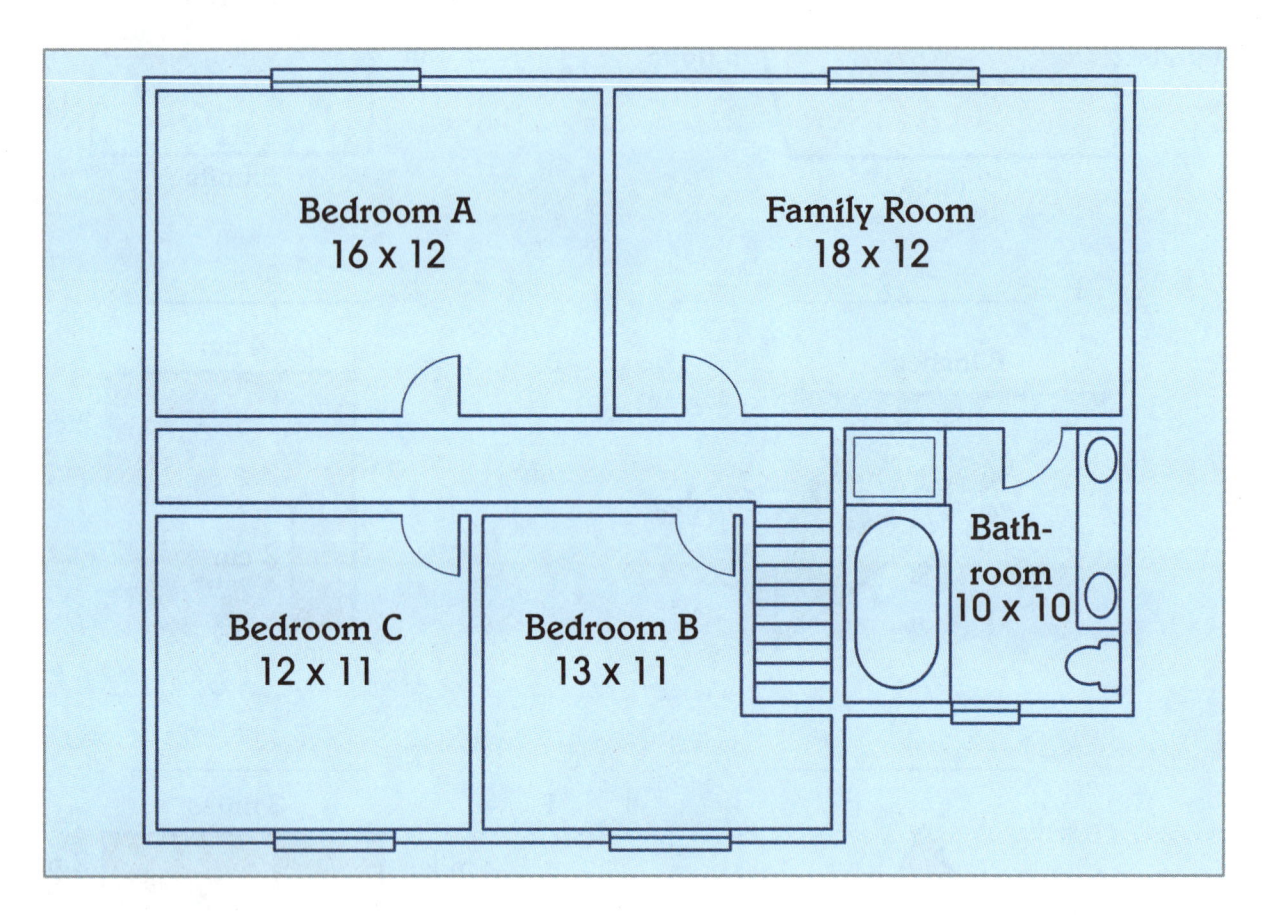

Bedroom A 16 x 12
Family Room 18 x 12
Bedroom C 12 x 11
Bedroom B 13 x 11
Bathroom 10 x 10

A. What is the area of the family room? _____ sq. ft.

B. How much larger is the family room than bedroom C? _____ sq. ft.

C. How many square feet do the 3 bedrooms total? _____ sq. ft.

D. What is the square footage of the bathroom? _____ sq. ft.

E. What is the total square footage of the entire upstairs? _____ sq. ft.

F. What is the difference in size between the largest bedroom and the bathroom? _____ sq. ft.

Perimeter and Area Practice

geometry

Remember: The perimeter is the distance around an object. Add the sides together to find the perimeter.

Remember: The area is the amount of square units within that object. Multiply the two sides of the object to find the area.

Study the example on page 81. Then, find the perimeter of each polygon.

A.

P = _____ cm

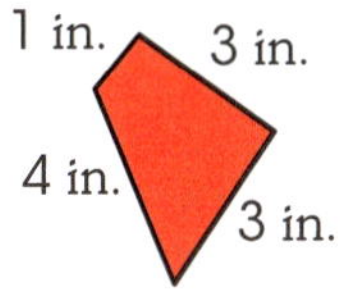

P = _____ in.

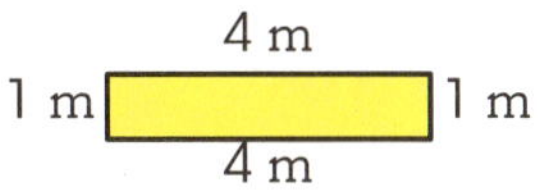

P = _____ m

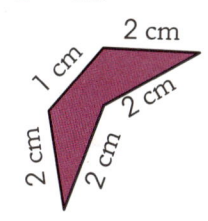

P = _____ cm

B.

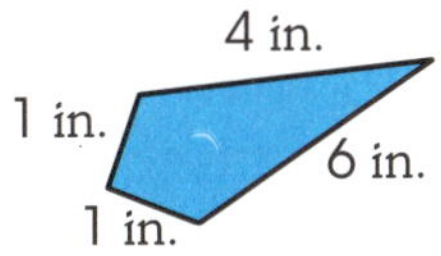

P = _____ in.

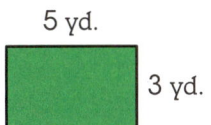

P = _____ yd.

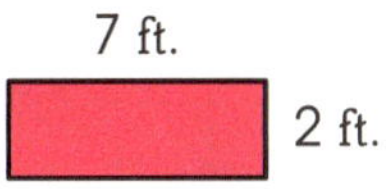

P = _____ ft.

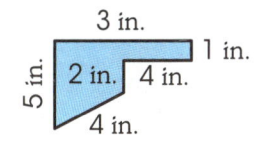

P = _____ in.

Study the example on page 82. Then, find the area of each polygon.

C.

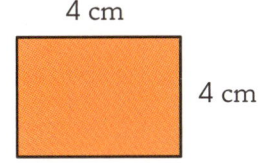

A = _____ sq. cm

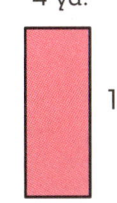

A = _____ sq. yd.

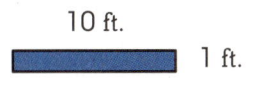

A = _____ sq. ft.

D.

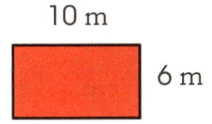

A = _____ sq. m

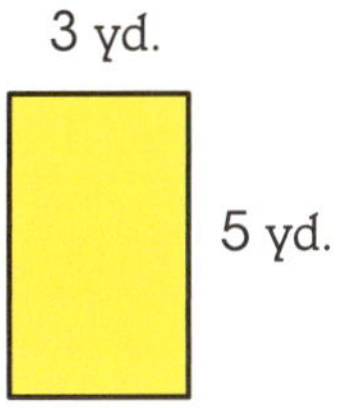

A = _____ sq. yd.

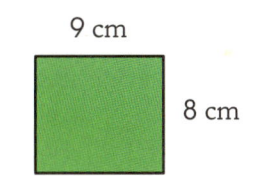

A = _____ sq. cm

Volume

geometry

You can find the **volume** by counting the cubic units that a figure contains. The volume is written in cubic units.
4 cm x 2 cm x 2 cm
= **16 cubic centimeters**

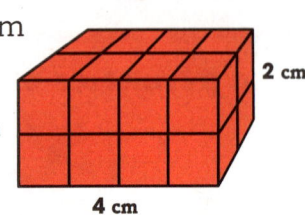

You can also multiply the length by the width by the height (l x w x h = v).
2 cm x 4 cm x 6 cm =
48 cubic centimeters

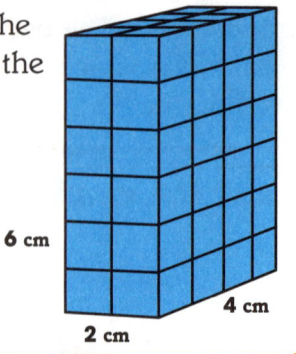

Study the examples above. Then, find the volume of each object.

A.
1 cm, 3 cm, 2 cm 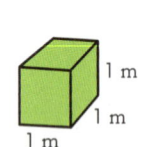 — _____ cu. cm 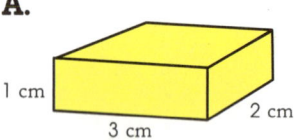
1 m, 1 m, 1 m 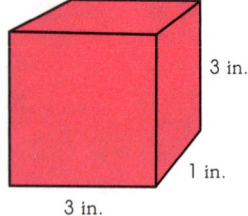 — _____ cu. m
3 in., 3 in., 1 in. — _____ cu. in.
1 m, 3 m, 2 m — _____ cu. m 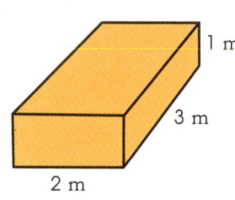

B.
4 ft., 2 ft., 2 ft. 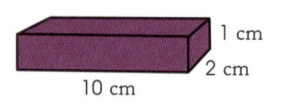 — _____ cu. ft. 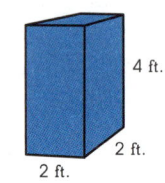
1 cm, 2 cm, 10 cm — _____ cu. cm
6 ft., 2 ft., 3 ft. — _____ cu. ft. 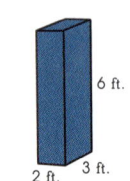

C.
4 cm, 3 cm, 1 cm 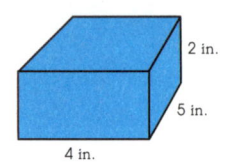 — _____ cu. cm 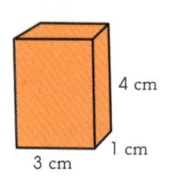
2 in., 5 in., 4 in. 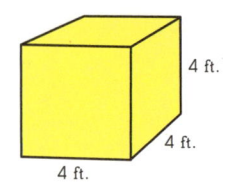 — _____ cu. in.
4 ft., 4 ft., 4 ft. — _____ cu. ft.
4 yd., 1 yd., 2 yd. — _____ cu. yd. 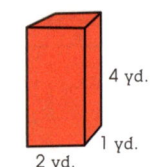

What is the total volume of this skyscraper model?

D. level 4 volume = _____ cu. in.

E. level 3 volume = _____ cu. in.

F. level 2 volume = _____ cu. in.

G. level 1 volume = _____ cu. in.

H. total volume = _____ cu. in.

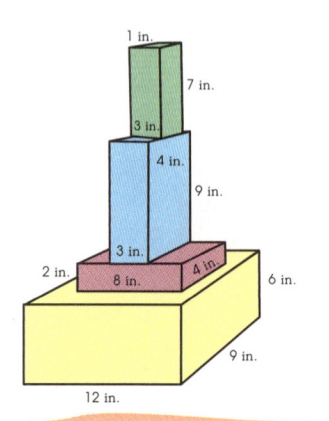

Addition and Subtraction

problem solving

> The problems on this page tell a story. Your job is to use information from the story to make a math problem and solve the problem. This is called **problem solving**.

Smoky Joe's Barbecue

MAIN DISHES	SIDE DISHES	BEVERAGES
Eye-Watering Ham ... $3.50	Flame Fries $1.10	Cola $0.75
Burning Hot Ribs $3.75	Sizzlin' Salad $1.05	Lemonade $0.85
Rockin' Roast Beef ... $4.25	Poppin' Potatoes $0.95	Milk $0.95

Study the menu above. Then, solve each problem.

A. Ariel ordered ribs and lemonade. How much will her lunch cost?

B. Michael ordered roast beef. He paid with a 5-dollar bill. How much change will he get?

C. Jonas has $4.08. He buys ham as a main dish. How much money does Jonas have left?

D. Terone wonders, "How much does an order of ribs, fries, and a cola cost?"

E. How much more is roast beef than milk?

F. Traci buys lemonade for herself and three friends. How much does she spend?

G. Ryan spent $5.55 for lunch. He got $0.45 back as change. How much did Ryan start out with?

H. Kelsey orders the least expensive item from each section of the menu. How much does she spend?

Multiplication

problem solving

Some story problems can be answered using multiplication. They ask you to find a total number. This is similar to addition. The difference is that these stories involve equal sets.

Example:

Matthew orders 3 ice cream cones. Each cone has 2 scoops. How many scoops of ice cream did Matthew order?

$$3 \times 2 = 6$$
number of sets — number in each set — total scoops

Study the example above. Then, solve each problem.

A. Gwen's 3 guinea pigs ate 24 seeds each. How many seeds did the guinea pigs eat?

B. We found 6 spider webs. Each web had trapped 17 bugs. How many bugs were trapped?

C. A ticket to the game costs $26.00. Amy wants to invite 4 friends. How much money does Amy need for tickets?

D. Our class ate 9 pizzas. Each pizza had 12 slices. How many slices of pizza did our class eat?

E. We passed 8 trucks on the highway. Each truck honked 4 times. How many honks did the trucks make in all?

F. Haley has 52 dimes in her bank. She has 39 nickels. How many coins does she have?

G. Jon is making lemonade for 16 people. Each glass needs 3 spoons of powdered mix. How many spoons of lemonade mix will Jon use?

H. Alonzo has 6 rolls of pennies. Each roll holds 50 pennies. How many pennies does Alonzo have?

Division

problem solving

Some story problems can be answered using division. They ask you to find missing parts or make smaller groups. They involve making equal sets, like these:

Example:

Yasmine had 9 hair ribbons. She split them evenly between 3 girls. How many ribbons did each girl get?

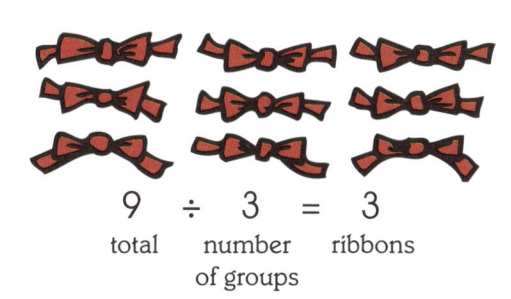

9 ÷ 3 = 3
total number ribbons
       of groups

Study the example above. Then, solve each problem.

A. The Millers have 6 children. When they come to the pool, they bring 36 toys that are equally shared. How many toys does each child get?

B. We found 11 flowers. Each one had 8 petals. How many petals does that make?

C. A car travels 120 miles in 3 hours. How many miles per hour does the car travel?

D. Mrs. Weitz passes out 24 papers equally to 8 students. How many papers does each child get?

E. Tara and Lacy share 12 cookies evenly. How many cookies does each girl get?

F. Luke is coloring eggs. Each container holds 12 eggs. Luke has 3 different colors. How many eggs can he color evenly per color?

G. There are 88 horse legs in the pasture. How many horses are there?

H. We looked under 5 rocks. We saw a total of 15 snails. How many snails were under each rock?

Choosing the Operation

problem solving

> Look for key words when deciding which operation to use. Here are a few examples of what to look for:
> **Addition:** How many are there **in all**, or **altogether**? **Example:** Teddy built 5 ship models. Bill built 4. How many do they have altogether?
> **Subtraction:** How many were **left**, or **leftover**, or **remaining**? What is the **difference**?
> **Example:** They started out with 200 books. They sold 140. How many are remaining?
> **Multiplication:** Look for the total of multiple groups. **Example:** The price for one ticket for the music festival is $2.00. What will 4 tickets cost? What will be the price for 7 tickets?
> **Division:** Look for the total given and the question asking for how many in each group.
> **Example:** If the total is 400 and there are 5 groups, how many are there in each group?

Write which operation you should use in each problem. Solve each problem.

A. Tom volunteered 3 Saturdays this month at the food bank. Ethan volunteered 4. Lenny wants to help others and volunteered 5 times! What is the total number of Saturdays they worked at the food bank?

Operation: _____

Answer: _____

B. This week, 27 girls signed up for ballet class. Last week, 16 girls signed up. How many more signed up this week?

Operation: _____

Answer: _____

C. A total of 200 students showed up for the bike rodeo on Saturday. Each of the 5 volunteers checked the same number of bikes to make sure they were safe. How many bikes did each volunteer check?

Operation: _____

Answer: _____

D. Mr. Bright was dunked 5 times by each of the 3 students that stepped up to see him plunge into the freezing cold water at the carnival! How many times was Mr. Bright dunked in all?

Operation: _____

Answer: _____

E. The carnival needed cakes for the cake walk. The 3rd grade brought 12, the 4th grade brought 23, and the 5th grade brought 14. How many cakes were brought in all?

Operation: _____

Answer: _____

F. There are 6 magnifying lenses in each bag. Mrs. Masters took out 7 bags so that each student could have one. How many lenses did she take out in all?

Operation: _____

Answer: _____

Too Much Information

problem solving

To solve word problems:
1. Decide which information is necessary to solve the problem.
2. Determine the operation.
3. Write a number sentence.
4. Solve.

Example: Andy brought 7 songs to play on guitar. Bill brought 6. They both brought 4 songs for the piano. How many songs did they bring in all for the guitar?
Needed information: Total songs brought for the guitar.
Operation: Addition
Number sentence: 7 + 6 =
Answer: **13 songs**

Study the example above. Then, solve each problem.

A. Mr. Rhodes asked his fourth-grade class how many of them owned kittens. He was amazed to find out that everyone raised their hands. The total amount of kittens was 44. He also found out that 25 dogs resided at these same homes. If there are 2 kittens per household, how many students are there in Mr. Rhodes's class?

Needed information:
Operation:
Number sentence:
Answer:

B. A total of 356 pounds of paper were collected for recycling by Mrs. Canup's class in the last 4 weeks. They also collected 289 pounds of cardboard. What is the average number of pounds of paper collected each week?

C. The Sandwich Shack was running a special. Sandwiches were only $0.49 on Wednesdays. Milkshakes were $0.89. Mr. Harland ordered 9 sandwiches for the students that did extra credit on their homework. How much did he pay for the sandwiches?

D. Maria's class has 4 pet mice in its classroom that the students love to play with every day. They also have 2 hamsters. Each mouse had 10 babies. How many mice does the class have now?

E. In the first week of school, 40 students at Hartsville Elementary School joined choir. Then, 50 students joined the band. In the second week, 25 more students joined the choir. What was the total number of students that joined the choir?

Time

problem solving

Solve each problem. Each problem is related to the one before, so complete them in order. Use A.M. and P.M. to specify the time of day.

A. Bryson gets up every morning at 6:30 A.M. It takes him 20 minutes to shower and get dressed. Then, he eats breakfast in 15 minutes. After breakfast, he does his chores. What time does Bryson start his chores?

_____

B. After breakfast and his bath, it takes Bryson 5 minutes to feed the dog. Then, he takes the dog for a walk for 30 minutes. What time is it now?

_____

C. Next, he sits down and reads for 45 minutes. Then, he leaves for school. What time is it when Bryson leaves?

_____

D. It takes Bryson 20 minutes to walk to school. What time does he get to school?

_____

E. He is at school for 6 and a half hours. Then, he walks home. What time should he get home from school? Remember, it took Bryson 20 minutes to walk to school.

_____

F. Bryson takes 5 minutes to change his clothes and 5 minutes to eat a snack. He rides his bike to soccer practice. It takes him 10 minutes to get there. What time does he arrive at practice?

_____

G. Soccer practice lasts 1 hour and 15 minutes. What time is soccer practice over?

_____

H. He rides his bike home with his friend. They talk for 23 minutes about the upcoming game. Then, Bryson puts his bike away, which takes 2 minutes. Next, he goes to the kitchen to help with dinner. What time is it now? Remember, it took him 10 minutes to ride to soccer practice.

_____

Summer Bridge Math RB-904088 © Rainbow Bridge Publishing

Money

problem solving

Solve each problem.

A. Marcella has 5 quarters and 3 nickels in her purse. She has $6.70 in her purse and her pocket altogether. What bills and coins does she have in her pocket?

B. Rachel has $8.53. She has 5 one-dollar bills and 1 quarter in her right hand. She does not have any bills in her left hand, just 10 coins. What coins does she have in her left hand that, together with the money in her right hand, total $8.53?

C. Robert has $7.92 in his money box. He has 3 bills and 12 coins in his box. He takes out 2 one-dollar bills and 1 quarter. What coins and bill does he have left in the box?

D. Peter's mother gave him 2 bills and 5 coins. He already had 6 one-dollar bills, 1 half-dollar, 1 dime, and 5 pennies. Now he has $17.47 in all. What kind of bills and coins did his mother give him?

E. Randy has 7 one-dollar bills in his wallet, 12 coins in his pocket, and 5 quarters, 3 nickels, 15 pennies, and 4 dimes at home on his dresser. He has $11.75 altogether. What 12 coins might he have in his pocket?

F. Miranda has 12 pennies, 6 quarters, 12 dimes, 2 half-dollars, 9 nickels, 1 ten-dollar bill, and 1 five-dollar bill in her piggy bank. How much money does she have in all?

Using a Pattern

problem solving

The best way to understand a pattern is to look at the difference between each number. Is there a pattern that follows all the numbers within the group?

Examples:

A. 7, 5, 3, 1 The pattern takes away 2 as it goes downward until it reaches 1.
B. 3, 7, 11, 15 The pattern adds 4 to each additional number.
C. 2, 4, 8, 16 The pattern multiplies each additional number by 2.

Identify each pattern. Then, solve each problem.

A. On Monday, Mr. Kosan gave out 3 problems for homework. Tuesday, he gave out 8 problems. On Wednesday, he assigned 13 problems. How many problems did he assign for Thursday and Friday?

B. Michael loves to share. On the first field day, he gave out 1 water bottle. The second day, he shared 3 bottles. The third day, he gave out 5 extra bottles of water. How many did he share on the fourth day if he continues this pattern?

C. The first week of the school fund-raiser, Emma sold 5 gifts. The second week, she sold 11 gifts. The third week, she sold 17. If this pattern continues, how many gifts will she sell the fifth week?

D. Andy loves to eat dates. He eats a few every day for lunch. The box started out with a total of 36. After the first day of lunch, there were 31 remaining. After the second day, there were 26. Continuing this same pattern, how many is he eating each day?

E. Mrs. Kline and Mr. Walker teamed up to have an after-school math club. The first week, only 1 person showed up for the club. The second week, 3 people showed up. The third week, 9 people showed up. How many students showed up the fourth week?

F. Angelica loves her puppy. Each day, she gives him 2 puppy treats while she trains him. If there are a total of 20 treats in the box, how many days will they last?

Answer Key

Page 7: A. 905, 730, 340, 172; **B.** 2,314; 1,170; 800; 512; **C.** 6,000; 4,000; 982; 960; **D.** 490, 472, 436, 401; **E.** 17, 71, 87, 107; **F.** 19, 96, 600, 906; **G.** 1,900; 2,700; 4,350; 7,000; **H.** 200, 620; 2,600; 6,200

Page 8: A. 9,000 + 500 + 10 + 6; **B.** 2,000 + 300 + 50 + 8; **C.** 1,000 + 400 + 0 + 7; **D.** 900 + 20 + 1; **E.** 7,000 + 800 + 0 + 0; **F.** 3,000 + 200 + 60 + 4; **G.** 5,000 + 100 + 80 + 2; **H.** 600 + 10 + 4; **I.** 4,000 + 0 + 70 + 3; **J.** 9,000 + 500 + 30 + 0

Page 9: A. 1,533; **B.** 5,947; **C.** 3,755; **D.** 7,479; **E.** 9,021; **F.** 3,102; **G.** 3,506; **H.** 6,098; **I.** 3,609; **J.** 1,698; **K.** 3,000 + 400 + 50 + 6; **L.** 7,000 + 300 + 20 + 4; **M.** 9,000 + 100 + 50 + 2; **N.** 3,000 + 500 + 60 + 9; **O.** 2,000 + 400 + 30 + 1; **P.** 4,000 + 0 + 20 + 2

Page 10: A. >, >, <; **B.** <, >, =; **C.** >, <, >; **D.** >, =, <; **E.** <, >, <; **F.** =, >, >; **G.** >, <; **H.** >, <

Page 11: A. 70, 10; **B.** 80, 50; **C.** 60, 60; **D.** 20, 30; **E.** 30, 100; **F.** 70, 40; **G.** 300, 600; **H.** 800, 700; **I.** 900, 400; **J.** 700, 200; **K.** 800, 400; **L.** 20,000; 70,000; 600,000; **M.** 4,000; 6,000; 8,000; **N.** 10,000, 4,000; 6,000; **O.** 40,000; 30,000; 6,000,000

Page 12: A. 85, 82, 90, 68, 28, 50; **B.** 635, 777, 949, 817, 368; **C.** 5,176; 3,216; 7,397; 1,777

Page 13: from left to right and top to bottom: 1,371; 631; 1,211; 1,492; 1,200; 658; 3,107; 1,156; 1,024; 4,053; 820; 1,033; 608; 603; 1,080; 706; A TAXICAB DRIVER!

Page 14: A. 93, 86, 133, 97, 132; **B.** 722, 615, 807, 860, 681; **C.** 679, 1,026; 1,166; 1,093; 1,056; **D.** 531, 478, 3, 293, 816; MATH IS A BLAST!

Page 15: A. 8,730; 7,821; 10,623; 4,415; **B.** 64,802; 5,546; 46,073; 43,563; **C.** 58,621; 96,442; 62,343; 73,332; **D.** 81,530; 106,008; 351,474; 693,477

Page 16: A. 26, 66, 18, 18, 56, 27; **B.** 742, 332, 472, 394, 331; **C.** 1,773; 1,780; 5,713; 5,913

Page 17: A. 366, 401, 122, 576; **B.** 173, 244; 1,764; 2,047; **C.** 6,722, 519; 2,853; 8,719; **D.** 4,109; 2,916; 7,884; 3,393

Page 18: A. 258, 256, 126, 264; **B.** 177, 488, 758; 3,596; **C.** 3,757; 1,463; 8,918; 1,886; **D.** 1,689; 1,778; 1,889; 3,856

Page 19: A. 2,338; 3,729; 1,589; 3,820; **B.** 8,858; 2,612; 8,768; 485; **C.** 3,805; 7,388; 5,321; 458; **D.** 774; 2,479; Answers will vary.

Page 20: Across: A. 2,535; **B.** 550,450; **C.** 5,350; **D.** 76,472; **E.** 19,290; **F.** 2,400; **G.** 27,305; **H.** 37,496; **Down: D.** 72,400; **I.** 38,225; **J.** 1,146; **K.** 35,225; **L.** 55,330; **M.** 4,220; **N.** 41,270; **O.** 72,090

Page 21: A. $1.43, $8.27, $70.61, $0.56; **B.** $0.93, $19.17, $604.07, $573.71; **C.** $361.00, $171.05, $270.42, $377.11; **D.** $42.17, $69.83, $85.10; A NEW BICYCLE!

Page 22: A. 16, 16; **B.** 9, 6; **C.** 6, 5; **D.** 3, 17; **E.** 15, 7; **F.** 13, 17; **G.** 13, 15; **H.** 12, 17; **I.** 15, 12; **J.** 14, 15; **K.** 16, 5; **L.** 12, 6; **M.** 7, 5

Page 23: A. 5 + 5 + 5 = 15, 5 x 3 = 15; **B.** 3 + 3 = 6, 3 x 2 = 6; **C.** 2 + 2 + 2 + 2 = 8, 2 x 4 = 8; **D.** 4 + 4 = 8, 4 x 2 = 8; **E.** 3 + 3 + 3 = 9, 3 x 3 = 9; **F.** 4 + 4 + 4 = 12, 4 x 3 = 12; **G.** 2 + 2 + 2 = 6, 2 x 3 = 6; **H.** 5 + 5 = 10, 5 x 2 = 10

Page 24: 1st riddle: YOUR RIGHT ELBOW!; **2nd riddle:** BECAUSE FISH HAVE THEIR OWN SCALES!

Page 25: A. 188, 189, 640, 126; **B.** 549, 144, 637, 208; **C.** 219, 360, 106, 355; **D.** 368, 189, 728, 164

Page 26: A. 728, 756; 1,062; 2,684; **B.** 1,500; 4,272; 878; 1,330; **C.** 900; 8,199; 708; 2,223; **D.** 1,488; 814; 1,155; 1,740

Page 27: A. 7,440; 14,420; 10,136; 17,220; **B.** 12,489; 12,546; 7,955; 26,244; **C.** 16,848; 28,764; 12,705; 9,614

Page 28: A. $55.43, $23.34, $7.14, $192.96; **B.** $46.23, $314.50, $37.74, $10.29; **C.** $45.36, $136.64, $89.04, $11.96; **D.** $26.04, $29.47, $19.80, $3.40

Page 29: A. five groups of two circled, 2; **B.** three groups of five circled, 5; **C.** three groups of two circled, 2; **D.** two groups of four circled, 4; **E.** three groups of three circled, 3; **F.** four groups of three circled, 3; **G.** six groups of two circled, 2; **H.** three groups of six circled, 6; **I.** seven groups of two circled, 2

Page 30: A. 16, 49, 18, 12; **B.** 15, 29, 12, 38; **C.** 14, 18, 24, 17

Page 31: A. 308 r1, 180 r4, 406 r1, 209 r3, 140 r5; **B.** 109 r2, 120 r6, 108 r2, 340, 190; **C.** 405 r1, 103 r4, 140 r5, 207 r1, 106 r5

Page 32: A. 813; 3,212; 984; 1,258; **B.** 867, 640, 852, 495; **C.** 547, 526, 198; 1,245

Page 33: A. 4 r2, 6 r2, 9 r4, 5 r2; **B.** 3 r2, 8 r2, 7 r5, 9 r2; **C.** 6 r3, 4 r3, 4 r4, 9 r7; **D.** 5 r6, 3 r5, 6 r6, 3 r3

Answer Key

Page 34: A. 428 r2; 3,421 r1, 284 r3, 216 r3; **B.** 412 r3, 634 r4, 385 r3; 3,122 r1; **C.** 452 r2, 247 r1; 4,234 r1, 467 r4

Page 35: A. 3 r3, 4 r2, 5 r10, 9 r7, 8 r4; **B.** 3 r43, 6 r10, 8 r20, 4 r4, 8 r12; **C.** 4 r26, 5 r9, 1 r80, 7 r20, 5 r10

Page 36: A. 6 x 5 = 30, 5 x 6 = 30, 30 ÷ 6 = 5, 30 ÷ 5 = 6; **B.** 3 x 8 = 24, 8 x 3 = 24, 24 ÷ 3 = 8, 24 ÷ 8 = 3; **C.** 4 x 3 = 12, 3 x 4 = 12, 12 ÷ 4 = 3, 12 ÷ 3 = 4; **D.** 2 x 7 = 14, 7 x 2 = 14, 14 ÷ 2 = 7, 14 ÷ 7 = 2; **E.** 2 x 8 = 16, 8 x 2 = 16, 16 ÷ 8 = 2, 16 ÷ 2 = 8; **F.** 4 x 7 = 28, 7 x 4 = 28, 28 ÷ 4 = 7, 28 ÷ 7 = 4

Page 37: A. 30, 10:00, 10:30; **B.** 15, 2:00, 2:15; **C.** 35, 7:00, 7:35; **D.** 55, 9:00, 9:55; **E.** 10, 8:00, 8:10; **F.** 50, 4:00, 4:50; **G.** 5, 10:00, 10:05; **H.** 45, 6:00, 6:45; **I.** 30, 5:00, 5:30; **J.** 5, 12:00, 12:05

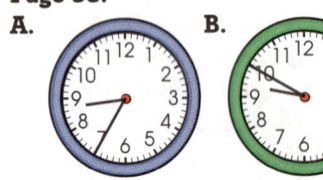

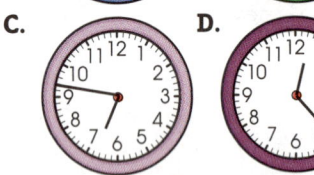

Page 38:
A. B.
C. D.
E. F.
G. H.

Page 38, continued
I.

Page 39: A. 8:00, 7:40, 11:35, 9:05; **B.** 1:32, 12:45, 6:55, 7:30; **C.** 10:45, 2:30, 3:00, 12:00

Page 40: A. $1.76; **B.** $1.03; **C.** $1.13; **D.** $4.00; **E.** $1.25; **F.** $2.00; **G.** $2.15; **H.** $2.50; **I.** $0.75; **J.** $3.05

Page 41: A. 1; **B.** 5; **C.** 4; **D.** 2; **E.** 20; **F.** 10; **G.** 10; **H.** 12; **I.** 15; **J.** 20; **K.–N.** Answers will vary.

Page 42: A. $3.90; **B.** $3.80; **C.** $4.05; **D.** $5.40; **E.** $0.50; **F.** $4.05; **G.** $0.85; **H.** $20.00; **I.** $0.81; **J.** $0.05; **K.** $2.51; **L.** $0.77

Page 43: A. $4.85; **B.** $10.90; **C.** $62.10; **D.** $31.80; **E.** $19.85; **F.–M.** Answers will vary.

Page 44: A. $\frac{1}{3}=\frac{2}{6}$, $\frac{1}{4}=\frac{2}{8}$, $\frac{1}{2}=\frac{3}{6}$; **B.** $\frac{3}{4}=\frac{6}{8}$, $\frac{2}{2}=1$, $\frac{1}{7}=\frac{2}{14}$; **C.** $\frac{1}{5}=\frac{2}{10}$, $\frac{1}{6}=\frac{2}{12}$, $\frac{8}{8}=1$; **D.** $\frac{2}{3}=\frac{6}{9}$, $\frac{2}{4}=\frac{8}{16}$, $\frac{1}{4}=\frac{3}{12}$; **E.** $\frac{1}{3}=\frac{2}{6}$, $\frac{2}{3}=\frac{4}{6}$, $\frac{1}{2}=\frac{5}{10}$

Page 45: A. $\frac{1}{3}<\frac{2}{3}$; **B.** $\frac{2}{4}=\frac{4}{8}$; **C.** $\frac{3}{8}<\frac{1}{2}$; **D.** $\frac{1}{3}=\frac{2}{6}$; **E.** $\frac{3}{4}>\frac{2}{4}$; **F.** $\frac{1}{2}<\frac{3}{4}$

Page 46: A. >, <, <, <; **B.** <, >, >, >; **C.** <, <, >, >; **D.** <, <, >, =; **E.** >, >, =, >

Page 47: A. $\frac{5}{6}$, $\frac{1}{4}$, $\frac{1}{3}$, $\frac{2}{3}$; **B.** $\frac{7}{8}$, $\frac{1}{3}$, $\frac{1}{3}$, $\frac{2}{5}$; **C.** $\frac{1}{2}$, $\frac{1}{3}$, $\frac{1}{2}$, $\frac{5}{8}$; **D.** $\frac{1}{2}$, $\frac{1}{2}$, $\frac{6}{7}$, $\frac{4}{5}$; **E.** $\frac{1}{4}$, $\frac{1}{4}$, $\frac{1}{5}$, $\frac{1}{4}$

Page 48: A. $2\frac{1}{7}$, $3\frac{1}{2}$, $1\frac{5}{8}$, $2\frac{1}{5}$; **B.** $1\frac{8}{9}$, $3\frac{1}{4}$, $5\frac{1}{5}$, $5\frac{1}{2}$; **C.** $2\frac{1}{2}$, $4\frac{1}{5}$, $3\frac{5}{6}$, $3\frac{1}{9}$; **D.** $4\frac{1}{2}$, $2\frac{1}{2}$, $4\frac{1}{3}$, $2\frac{1}{4}$; **E.** $1\frac{2}{7}$, $7\frac{1}{2}$, $2\frac{4}{5}$, $2\frac{1}{6}$

Page 49: A. $\frac{3}{4}$, $\frac{2}{5}$, $\frac{4}{5}$; **B.** $\frac{9}{10}$, $\frac{2}{8}$, $\frac{6}{10}$; **C.** $\frac{8}{9}$, $\frac{7}{12}$, $\frac{1}{4}$; **D.** $\frac{80}{100}$, $\frac{78}{100}$, $\frac{100}{100}$

Page 50: A. $\frac{3}{10}$, $\frac{3}{4}$, $\frac{9}{14}$, $\frac{11}{15}$; **B.** $\frac{5}{6}$, $\frac{7}{8}$, $\frac{5}{8}$, $\frac{9}{14}$; **C.** $\frac{7}{10}$, $\frac{7}{12}$, $\frac{9}{10}$, $\frac{3}{4}$; **D.** $\frac{7}{12}$, $\frac{4}{5}$, $\frac{5}{16}$, 1

Page 51: A. $\frac{1}{4}$, $\frac{2}{3}$, $\frac{3}{10}$, $\frac{3}{14}$; **B.** $\frac{1}{6}$, $\frac{1}{4}$, $\frac{3}{8}$, $\frac{1}{10}$; **C.** $\frac{3}{18}$, $\frac{1}{12}$, 0, $\frac{1}{4}$; **D.** $\frac{1}{4}$, $\frac{1}{10}$, $\frac{1}{14}$, $\frac{3}{8}$

Page 52: A. 5, 2, 5, 5; **B.** 2, 3, 4, 9; **C.** 6, 5, 9, 4; **D.** 9, 14, 8, 2; **E.** 4, 9, 8, 15

Page 53: from left to right and top to bottom: 0.8 (blue), 0.15 (green), 0.73 (green), 0.36 (green), 0.81 (green), 0.1 (blue), 0.7 (blue), 0.6 (blue), 0.4 (blue), 0.9 (blue)

Page 54: A. 0.5, 1.4, 2.8, 3.7; **B.** 4.1, 5.8, 6.3, 7.9; **C.** 0.1, 0.7, 1.3, 1.6; **D.** 0.3, 0.8, 1.9, 2.4; **E.** 0.5, 2.8, 3.1, 3.6; **F.** 1.4, 2.1, 2.6, 2.8

Page 55: A. >, <, >, <; **B.** <, <, >, >; **C.** >, >, <, >; **D.** <, <, <, <; **E.** >, >, >, <; **F.** <, >, >, <; **G.** >, <, <, >; **H.** >, >, >, >

Page 56: A. 4, 7, 11, 6; **B.** 21, 11, 5, 14; **C.** 9, 8, 9, 11; **D.** 10, 10, 8, 7; **E.** 2, 13, 1, 5; **F.** 6.3, 10.7, 14.8, 6.8; **G.** 3.5, 24.4, 17.5, 28.2; **H.** 5.5, 10.4, 3.6, 6.3; **I.** 17.6, 112.3, 9.4, 400.7; **J.** 18.3, 320.8, 62.0, 78.5

Page 57: Across: A. 25.63; **B.** 11.55; **C.** 4.7; **D.** 10.5; **E.** 5.30; **F.** 1.10; **G.** 8.34; **H.** 2.2; **Down: A.** 25.33; **C.** 4.03; **D.** 1.01; **I.** 68.61; **J.** 5.59; **K.** 7.52; **L.** 1.73; **M.** 28.12; **N.** 41.23

Page 58: Across: A. 11.7; **B.** 0.4; **C.** 3.9; **D.** 2.8; **E.** 22.2; **F.** 3.13; **G.** 4.46; **H.** 5.6; **I.** 1.7; **J.** 0.9; **Down: A.** 15.2; **B.** 0.3; **F.** 3.63; **I.** 10.9; **K.** 1.61; **L.** 2.7; **M.** 9.33; **N.** 8.2; **O.** 2.47; **P.** 1.53

Page 59: A. 2.3, 1.2, 0.64, 6.2, 2.4; **B.** 5.6, 3.18, 2.74, 0.83, 7.6; **C.** 3.02, 3.87, 13.16, 4.46, 1.1; **D.** 3.36, 3.37, 4.36, 7.2, 20.86; **E.** 0.6, 3.05, 3.54, 7.75, 11.12

Answer Key

Page 60: A. $\frac{4}{10}$, 0.4; **B.** $\frac{2}{10}$, 0.2; **C.** $\frac{5}{10}$, 0.5; **D.** $1\frac{4}{10}$, 1.4; **E.** $1\frac{1}{10}$, 1.1; **F.** $2\frac{9}{10}$, 2.9

Page 61: A. $\frac{21}{100}$, 0.21; **B.** $\frac{47}{100}$, 0.47; **C.** $\frac{34}{100}$, 0.34; **D.** $\frac{69}{100}$, 0.69; **E.** $1\frac{7}{100}$, 1.07; **F.** $1\frac{2}{100}$, 1.02; **G.** $2\frac{4}{100}$, 2.04; **H.** $\frac{1}{100}$, 0.01

Page 62: A. >, >, >; **B.** =, <, >; **C.** >, =, =; **D.** <, <, >; **E.** <, >, <; **F.** oz., t., gal., oz.; **G.** c., gal., lb., gal.; **H.** 48; 4,000; 8; **I.** 4, 6, 6; **J.** 80, 10, 32

Page 63: A. 5,000; 3,000; 8,000; 1,000; **B.** 7,000; 9,000; 2,000; 11,000; **C.** 500 mL; 1,000 mL; 20 mL; **D.** 15 mL, 120 L, 4 L; **E.** 5 mL; 80,000 L; 400 mL; **F.** 255 mL, 17 mL, 10 mL

Page 64: A. g, kg, g, g; **B.** kg, g, g; **C.** 60 kg, 11g, 1 kg; **D.** 15g, 30g, 10g, 7 kg

Page 65: A. 2.5; **B.** 3.5; **C.** 2; **D.** 0.5; **E.** 3; **F.** 5.5; **G.** 36, 9, 3,520; **H.** 120; 21,120; 15; **I.** 96; 84; 30; **J.** 5,280; 6; 18; **K.** in., yd., in., mi.; **L.** yd., ft., in., yd.

Page 66: A. m; **B.** km; **C.** cm; **D.** km; **E.** km; **F.** m; **G.** cm; **H.** m; **I.** cm; **J.** cm; **K.** 8,000; 4; **L.** 10,000; 6,000; **M.** 500; 7,000; **N.** 2,000; 9,000; **O.** 700; 100,000

Page 67: A. 4th; **B.** 5th; **C.** 3,100 lbs.; **D.** 500 lbs.; **E.** 6th; **F.** 100; **G.** 6th; **H.** June; **I.** 20; **J.** April; **K.** 20; **L.** 160; **M.** Sept.; **N.** 60

Page 68: A. beets, peas; **B.** broccoli; **C.** yellow squash; **D.** beans; **E.** broccoli; **F.** yellow squash; **G.** broccoli; **H.** Dec.; **I.** Feb., Mar.; **J.** Nov., Dec.; **K.** 20; **L.** Oct., Mar.; **M.** 44

Page 69: A. (1, 1), (3, 4); **B.** (4, 5), (7, 1); **C.** (1, 3), (8, 3); **D.** (3, 1), (6, 3); **E.** (4, 2), (7, 4); **F.** M, H, L, T; **G.** A, H, P, H; **H.** T, E, S, E; **I.** Y, P; **J.** O, O; **K.** U, I; **L.** G, N; **M.** E, T; **N.** T, !; **message:** MATH HELPS YOU GET THE POINT!

Page 70: A. 75, 40, 200, 100, 80; **B.** 100, 0, 50, 25, 85; **C.** j., e.; **D.** f., c.; **E.** d., b.; **F.** i., g.; **G.** h., a.

Page 71: A. Th; **B.** 4; **C.** 4; **D.** Monday, March 19; **E.** Saturday, March 31; **F.** Th; **G.** March 27; **H.** W; **I.** F; **J.** July 31; **K.** 2; **L.** July 15; **M.** Wednesday, July 25; **N.** July 14

Page 72: A. yes, yes, yes, no, yes; **B.** yes, no, no, yes, no; **C.** yes, yes, yes, yes, no; **D.–E.** Check lines of symmetry.

Page 73: A. square, rectangle, trapezoid, rhombus; **B.** square, rhombus; **C.** triangle; **D.** circle; **E.** pentagon; **F.** hexagon; **G.** octagon; **H.** square, rectangle, trapezoid, rhombus, hexagon, octagon; **I.** A rhombus has 2 sets of parallel lines. A trapezoid has only 1 set of parallel lines.

Page 74: A. quadrilateral, triangle, triangle, pentagon; **B.** quadrilateral, triangle, pentagon, pentagon; **C.** quadrilateral, triangle, quadrilateral, pentagon; **D.** square, parallelogram, rectangle, parallelogram

Page 75: yes, yes

Page 76: A. flip; **B.** no; **C.** turn; **D.** slide; **E.** no; **F.** flip; **G.** turn; **H.** flip; **I.** flip

Page 77: A. pyramid, cylinder, sphere, cone; **B.** cube, rectangular prism, pyramid, sphere; **C.** cylinder, pyramid, rectangular prism, cube; **D.** cone, cone, sphere, cone

Page 78: A. ray CD, line LM, segment XY, line AB; **B.** segment BC, line ST, ray EF, ray DE; **C.** intersecting, parallel, perpendicular, parallel; **D.** Check line drawings.

Page 79: A. acute, right, obtuse; **B.** right, obtuse, acute; **C.** acute, obtuse, right; **D.** obtuse; Angles will vary.

Page 80: from left to right and top to bottom: 4, 4, 4, yes, no; 3, 3, 3, no, no; 4, 4, 4, yes, no; 0, 0, 0, no, yes; 4, 4, 4, yes, yes; 5, 5, 5, no, no; 1, 2, 0, no, no

Page 81: A. 24 units; **B.** 10 units; **C.** 24 inches; **D.** 16 cm; **E.** 21 miles; **F.** 32 miles

Page 82: A. 216; **B.** 84; **C.** 467; **D.** 100; **E.** 783; **F.** 92

Page 83: A. 14, 11, 10, 9; **B.** 12, 16, 18, 19; **C.** 16, 40, 10; **D.** 60, 15, 72

Page 84: A. 6, 48, 9, 6; **B.** 16, 20, 6; **C.** 12, 40, 64, 8; **D.** 21; **E.** 108; **F.** 64; **G.** 648; **H.** 841

Page 85: A. $3.75 + $0.85 = $4.60; **B.** $5.00 − $4.25 = $0.75; **C.** $4.08 − $3.50 = $0.58; **D.** $3.75 + $1.10 + $0.75 = $5.60; **E.** $4.25 − $0.95 = $3.30; **F.** $0.85 + $0.85 + $0.85 + $0.85 = $3.40; **G.** $5.55 + $0.45 = $6.00; **H.** $3.50 + $0.95 + $0.75 = $5.20

Answer Key

Page 86: A. 3 x 24 = 72 seeds;
B. 6 x 17 = 102 bugs;
C. $26.00 x 5 = $130.00;
D. 9 x 12 = 108 slices;
E. 8 x 4 = 32 honks;
F. 52 + 39 = 91 coins;
G. 16 x 3 = 48 spoons;
H. 6 x 50 = 300 pennies

Page 87: A. 36 ÷ 6 = 6 toys;
B. 11 x 8 = 88 petals;
C. 120 ÷ 3 = 40 miles;
D. 24 ÷ 8 = 3 papers;
E. 12 ÷ 2 = 6 cookies;
F. 12 x 4 = 48 eggs;
G. 88 ÷ 4 = 22 horses;
H. 5 x 3 = 15 snails

Page 88: A. addition, 3 + 4 + 5 = 12 Saturdays; **B.** subtraction, 27 − 16 = 11 girls; **C.** division, 200 ÷ 5 = 40 bikes; **D.** multiplication, 5 x 3 = 15 times; **E.** addition, 12 + 23 + 14 = 49 cakes; **F.** multiplication, 6 x 7 = 42 lenses

Page 89: A. students in Mr. Rhodes's class, division, 44 ÷ 2 = 22 students; **B.** average pounds of paper collected each week, division, 356 ÷ 4 = 89 pounds of paper; **C.** how much Mr. Harland paid for the sandwiches, multiplication, 9 x 0.49 = $4.41; **D.** how many mice does the class have now, multiplication and addition, 4 x 10 = 40 babies, 40 babies + 4 parents = 44 total mice; **E.** total number of students that joined choir, addition, 40 + 25 = 65 students

Page 90: A. 7:05 A.M.; **B.** 7:40 A.M.; **C.** 8:25 A.M.; **D.** 8:45 A.M.; **E.** 3:20 P.M.; **F.** 3:50 P.M.; **G.** 5:05 P.M.; **H.** 5:40 P.M.

Page 91: A. 2 one-dollar bills, 3 quarters, 1 nickel; **B.** 6 half-dollars, 1 quarter, 3 pennies; **C.** 1 five-dollar bill, 6 dimes, 1 nickel, 2 pennies; **D.** 2 five-dollar bills, 1 half-dollar, 1 quarter, 1 nickel, 2 pennies; **E.** Answers will vary.; 2 half-dollars, 6 quarters, 6 nickels or 4 half-dollars, 8 dimes; **F.** $19.22

Page 92: A. 3, 8, 13, add 5 each day, Thursday = 18, Friday = 23; **B.** 1, 3, 5, add 2 each day, 4th day = 7 bottles; **C.** 5, 11, 17, add 6 each day, 5th week = 29 gifts; **D.** 36, 31, 26, subtract 5 each day, eat 5 each day; **E.** 1, 3, 9, multiply by 3 each week, 4th week = 27 students; **F.** add 2 each day until reaches 20, 10 days